# DARE TO BE TRUE
## NO PLEASURE IS COMPARABLE
## TO THE STANDING UPON
## THE VANTAGE-GROUND OF TRUTH
### *Francis Bacon 1561-1626*

# CONTENTS

# FOREWORD

*Estranged: adjective (of a person) no longer close or affectionate to someone; alienated.* Oxford Dictionary

At least one-third of families in the UK are currently estranged from family members and we do not know for sure how many children, siblings, parents, cousins and grandparents globally are living with an estrangement. Here are just a few names in the media currently experiencing this ever-growing problem:

- Nicole Kidman
- Ryan O'Neal
- Mia Farrow
- Tom Cruise
- Billy Ray Cyrus
- Martin Sheen
- Jackie Chan
- Curtis James Jackson
- Woody Allen
- Warren Buffet
- Kelly Rowland
- Lindsay Lohan
- Marshal Mathers 'Eminem'
- Beyoncé
- Courtney Love
- Christina Aguilera
- Meg Ryan
- Kate Hudson
- Drew Barrymore

- Rosanne Barr
- Ariana Grande
- Justin Beiber
- Jennifer Aniston
- Steven Spielberg
- Macaulay Culkin
- Michael Jackson
- Adele
- Demi Lovato
- Kate Hudson
- Drew Barrymore
- Jay-Z
- Meghan Markle
- Anthony Hopkins

The list grows and one thing is for sure if you are estranged ... you are not alone.

References: Wikipedia2020/NinjaJournalist2020

It is estimated that over five million people in the UK are estranged from a family member, but despite being so common it is not something that is widely known about or discussed. Over 9000 students at UK Universities are estranged from their families, leaving them financially, materially and emotionally vulnerable during their studies. These talented, committed young people may be up to three times more likely to drop out of University as a result.

Ref: Family Estrangement and the COVID-19 Crisis: A closer look at how broken family relationships have been impacted by the COVID-19 crisis. Report by Dr Lucy Blake (Edge Hill University), Dr Becca Bland (Stand Alone), Dr Sarah Foley and Dr Susan Imrie (Centre for Family Research, University of Cambridge). June 22nd, 2020

# DEDICATION

*This book is dedicated to the grandchildren I hope to know one day and Caraline Neville-Lister. A magazine article showed pictures of her and her pathetic body. Caraline was 29 years old and the article was promoting the BBC2 '40 Minutes' TV programme highlighting her shocking life. She was suffering from extreme symptoms of anorexia nervosa and had said "I want to be thin, but it's not to do with magazines and models. I want to be as slim as a shadow so nobody can hurt me anymore. I want to take up as little space as possible. Her past was riddled with harrowing stories of how her mother had treated both Caraline and her six brothers and sisters with serious neglect and abuse. The consequences for her, and probably her siblings too, were to grow up only feeling as worthless as humanly possible and to show the world in the most natural way, by starving herself.*

*I was compelled to write to her and tell her my story, thankfully nowhere near as severe as hers, although I was near to anorexic myself at the time. In my mind I had been near to where Caraline was and thought my support might help.*

*I contacted the magazine's offices and they said they would be happy to send my letter to her along with the others, as they had received a huge response to the article. Whether she read my letter I will never know. I very much doubt it. Caraline died shortly after the programme was aired. Intelligent and logically minded, the one thing she could not break through was the conditioning both her mother and society had drilled into her mind 'You can trust your mother's judgement.'*

*That's fine when you are blessed with a mother who understands the part she plays in your life. For the right reasons, to help you grow and blossom and bring out the best in you. But sadly not all mothers are like that. In fact, it seems there are more and more victims living through damage from mothers than ever before. Perhaps emotional abuse is a better description than damage.*

*People like Caraline were emotionally abused, no doubt about it. So conditioned with "mother knows best" they relied on that way of thinking to know where their place in life was. And because we trust our mothers implicitly, we never question the place they give us in the world. But their idea of 'you' is not necessarily correct.*

*To constantly to be told your place is nowhere, hurts. The emotional pain endured is far worse than any physical pain and because it's inflicted by someone you trust, a figure of authority, you feel you must believe them.*

*This author knew so well just how Caraline was feeling. She too only wanted to exist with no fuss. Her mother was her authority and so she should be. Or so she thought.*

Ref: TV Quick Magazine 1994

# A NOTE FROM THE AUTHOR

Anyone suffering the effects of an estrangement with a close family member knows this is personal and private, feeling stigmatised and can experience anything from despair to shame. No ethnicity, race, colour, creed, caste, religion or even a member of royalty is immune from this condition. The pain of missing a loved one is constantly exacerbated by the portrayal of happy families in the media and just seeing a mother walking arm in arm with her adult daughter in the park can be distressing for some sufferers. Each and every version of a family estrangement is unique and can last for so many years that the often vague or sometimes unknown reason for the initial falling out may be lost in time. For some, the rift may be short-lived when the people involved get the chance to thrash out their differences, making amends, forgiving and forgetting. While for others there is simply no opportunity for the stalemate to be overcome and the years pass with no movement or contact on either side.

Sometimes misplaced loyalty can go unnoticed for decades and what we innocently believed was the right thing to do only now exposes how terribly wrong our judgement may have been. This is the true story of one person's life which, when examined closely, highlights the very thing that perpetuates the estrangements to come. It might be too late to put things that happened in the past right but counting losses can be much more beneficial than we can possibly imagine.

No academic or other qualification attained anywhere in the world can prepare us for the change a family estrangement will make to our lives and in order to validate my authority on this subject I put before you my own personal experience which I hope assures the reader how familiar I am with the emotional pain, distress and sadness of family rifts. I had doubts about my own sanity for a very long time but now I have found my voice and I'm not afraid to use it. This is a factual account of what happened to me and I have only changed the names involved because apportioning blame is of no importance.

I hope this book helps give you the strength and courage needed to understand what most likely happened, without you even being aware of it at the time, and how you can now recover from a most unnatural circumstance you may, unfortunately, find yourself in.

SANDY GRAYSON

# CHAPTER ONE

# DUTY CALLS

At 7pm the mother walked to her car parked some way down the street while her teenage daughters were taking time to get ready to be chauffeured to yet another friends' house for another evening's fun. As she opened the door she felt the warmth where the setting sun had been resting on the windscreen. She always enjoyed the tranquil peace and sumptuous pleasure of being enveloped in that warmth. She loved that car. It was the only possession that was hers after the recent divorce and it was a special time of day in late summer when, even in an East London side street there was a magical yellow glaze over everything. She had no plans herself and certain that patience was a virtue was happy to wait, bringing along her new self-help book, perfect for these quiet moments. She had read so many, looking for the illusive answer. She'd had more 'therapy' than most. Psychology, Psychiatry, Mind Counselling, Cognitive Behavioural Therapy, Herbology, Homeopathy, Reflexology, Palmistry, Spiritual Healing and Clairvoyant readings. You name it, she'd had it. But she didn't know what was actually wrong with her or how she could overcome whatever it was. Before reaching the second page she put the book down, discarding it permanently, probably to be dropped into Claire's charity shop in the High Street tomorrow. She had no interest in how to improve herself when an author mentioned in the opening pages their thanks to parents or children or whoever for help with the book. No author could possibly understand what she needed if they were just academically qualified. She needed an author who had been through similar experiences and one that had come out better the other end. She had no idea it would, some years later, be her.

Dutifully waiting, she turned the radio on more out of curiosity than habit. The girls usually chose the channel. It was easier than trying to argue. Even at forty-four she preferred not to select a radio station and come to think of it, if she was honest which was the one thing she knew she most certainly was, she wasn't really comfortable making most decisions now her offspring were so capable and sure of themselves. She was so proud of them. She had, if nothing else, at least produced two beautiful daughters who were nothing short of 'formidable.' But this was a rare treat. It was a phone-in. How interesting. What was the subject? The female caller said just a few words and in a moment the mother instantly picked up on the subject, 'Aha, lack of self-esteem, that was easy to deduce.' The woman's voice sounded older than expected and she was shocked when the caller, speaking in a noticeably hesitant whisper stated she was sixty-one, describing to the DJ therapist her lack of self-confidence. The mother couldn't believe someone of THAT age could still be living with the problems SHE hoped to resolve well before reaching sixty-one. Somehow the answer now seemed more elusive than ever.

The mother, Georgia, had recently divorced her husband of nineteen years and had quickly realised it would have made no difference to her 'hang ups' if she had stayed married to him. But what relief though... no more him shouting at her and no more controlling. She remembered the Police song 'Every Breath You Take' and how she had related to the words, 'I'll be watching you.' "Not anymore you won't! Phew!" She remembered the shocking similarities when she had watched the film Sleeping With

*The Enemy.* She knew the road ahead wouldn't be easy but considering her options, she felt lucky to still be alive and intact. The girls would understand in time. Georgia was from a broken home herself and was sure everything would be better this time. It was one confidence she never doubted.

# CHAPTER TWO

# THE BOX

It's just a box, a simple, large, cardboard box. Ok, it had been in the garage unopened for more than twelve years and why now was she ready to remember everything inside it? And why was she feeling so happy while quietly going about the business of tidying and cleaning the place when these chores were only done when visitors were imminent? After all, she was a sixty-one year-old woman living in the Twenty First Century with no old-fashioned ideas like 'keeping the place spick and span because you never know when the Queen might come to visit', aha echoes of mum there. She was a free spirit now, unconventional and quite radical at times, only doing things that made her happy. She had a busy life, so why was she giving herself extra work to do when it was her who brought the box indoors wanting to go through it?

She knew what was in it. She put it all there. No one else knew what it contained because she had abandoned any idea of sharing its contents years ago. She'd tried so many times before but felt so small talking about something that no one else had the vaguest idea of and certainly had no interest in. She knew her words would be lost before they'd even left her lips. But now is different. Now she was a proper grown-up, older, wiser, heavier too and she knew the importance of sharing the facts with whoever was prepared to believe her, sharing the things she and others did wrong. As they say you can't make it up, the truth, that is.

Over the years she had forgotten about the book in that box, the book she had written. The change of addresses and husbands didn't help her remember exactly where it was either. She knew it had been in the garage all these years and had thought of it as 'cathartic writing,' never giving it a thought anymore until today. But today was different. Today was the 'Find that box in the garage' day, thanks to her new friend Jane who she'd met on her latest working cruise. Georgia was now a guest speaker and craft instructor for a cruise company, travelling around the world in style with what she jokingly called 'her current husband' Tony. Georgia had hit it off with Jane immediately when they were at the Muster Station just before casting off from Tilbury on a tour of the British Isles. Jane had helped her untangle the life jacket and got it over her head and ship shape in no time. Tony and Will, Jane's husband, were like old friends and enjoyed some hilarious moments together on and off the ship, like when they all shared the hire car that took the four of them to Invergordon where Jane had bought laid back Will a ginger wig attached to a tartan beret with a red pom-pom, which he wore the entire day. And what about the phantom urinator? They had spied a man way off in the distance and as they got closer, found the evidence. They were sure Urquhart Castle, Loch Ness and Inverness High Street had never seen four people falling about in such hysterics before. They promised to meet up again after the cruise and a month later they did.

Tony and Georgia knew they were lucky to have this kind of life on board. With passenger status, they were meeting new people and seeing wonderful sights around the world. It was after she had confided in Jane about her situation back home that they agreed they had a common factor. Jane's ex-daughter-in-law was making it difficult for her and Will to see their granddaughter. A painful estrangement.

It was only yesterday they had all met up for lunch at Pizza Express at the shopping centre when she had told Jane about writing the book years ago and the events of the past, "but there is no point in continuing with it," Georgia said. "My mother would have me in court in seconds for libel." It was one of those life defining moments as Jane quickly snapped back, "Your mother would have to *prove you wrong*. You have the facts and she would have to prove *them* wrong too!" she insisted.

But Georgia had left the facts behind so long ago and had built herself a new life, having been forced to leave all that she knew buried until mentioning the book yesterday. Yesterday was an historic day in itself. It was 21st of July 2015 and Neil Armstrong walked on the moon exactly forty-six years earlier. She remembered with crystal clear vision precisely where she was all those years ago and why....

In 1969 Georgia was fifteen years old and could hardly contain her excitement at the prospect of witnessing the biggest event the world had ever seen. She'd followed every news article she could find and knew all the statistics there was to know about the moon landing. She had been looking forward to this moment for months, but a week earlier she had been an emergency admission at Hackney Hospital and would have to remain there when the landing was being televised. She'd had an epileptic fit while working on the egg stall in Well Street Market. She lived just up the road above a local shop and sold eggs on the market stall every Saturday. She was a schoolgirl and remembers the mess she had made by accidentally dropping most of the eggs she picked up while trying to put them in their boxes. When she came round she was lying on the cold pavement surrounded by lots of staring faces and feeling her wet head, she looked round to quickly realise it was raw egg. There was egg over her bare arms, legs, clothes, even inside the heel of her shoes. She thought 'God only knows what I must have looked like when I hit the ground,' and fifteen-year-old girls are only concerned with what they look like. What an embarrassment she was. What a sight she must have been in the crowded marketplace. 'What must they have thought of her as she lay there dazed and confused on the ground between the shops and the stalls. Saturday was the busiest market day and it was also mini-skirt days. Suddenly alarmed, 'Had anyone seen her knickers?' She didn't remember much after regaining consciousness except the ambulance taking her to the hospital, where she now was. Could she ever face the locals again?

Epilepsy's a funny thing she knew nothing about it as a teenager and certainly didn't know that the twitching of her hands, then arms and legs that flung her into the air at the most inappropriate times and places would cause the kind of embarrassment and physical pain that it did. Her mother didn't know anything about the condition either. Months before the first convulsion, when she asked why her hand was jumping out of control, her mother would say she was 'attention seeking' or 'you're a hypochondriac.' Well, mums know best don't they? She loved her mother and never felt the need to question her, trusting her judgement implicitly.

Georgia was comfortable enough in the adult ward. The bed rails on either side seemed very high, so she didn't fall out, she supposed. She was afraid of the dark room they took her to on several occasions where they put wires on her head and flashed lights into her eyes. No one explained anything. It was all a mystery and she was scared.

It didn't take long for her to notice there was no TV back in the ward and so worried she might miss the moon landing asked one of the nurses if it was possible to watch it on a TV *anywhere in the hospital.* She told her the day and time it was going to be televised and walking away, the nurse said 'Ok, I'll do my best.' And the nurse didn't forget. Undoing the bed rails, she motioned Georgia to climb into a wheelchair, put a blanket across her lap and proceeded to take her along lots of long corridors, in and out of a lift and into a vast, cold and empty ward. At the far end of the room she could just make out a tiny black and white TV bolted high up on the wall. The nurse said 'I'll come back later for you' and from 8pm Georgia sat alone in the cold room, totally mesmerized by what she witnessed that evening. It was truly special. Thank you nurse.

There was an epic event occurring back home too. Georgia's mother had just discovered her husband was having an affair with one of her best friends. The ensuing fights and heartache were never far away from Georgia's mind and she did wonder, could stress induce epilepsy?

The consultant neurologist had suggested it was a likely cause although her mother dismissed the idea as 'rubbish'.

The family had moved just a mile away from the council flat in Homerton a couple of years earlier to a small shop attached to a two-bedroom maisonette and coming home from school one day, she walked in to find her Aunt Mary waiting for her. *'Your father's had an accident and I'm taking you home to stay with us for a while'* was all she said. Georgia's questions were brushed aside as if irrelevant and she was left to imagine what on earth had happened. Here's what actually happened...

Georgia's father owned a ladies' coat factory and had been in Bethnal Green on business one afternoon and crossing the busy Cambridge Heath Road couldn't have been concentrating much on the traffic as the wing mirror of a passing post office van caught his face as he stepped off the pavement. He had sustained serious head injuries and an ambulance had rushed him to the Royal London Hospital in Whitechapel just a few miles away from the accident, where he was given an emergency tracheotomy which saved his life. He lost a whole load of teeth and had major surgery to put his face back together again, which was eventually revealed to Georgia many weeks later when she and her mother were escorted by a nurse into a small and very dark room. There was no sound at all and there was nothing in the room except one bed, and as they stood there Georgia felt her heart pound as she saw her father's unshaven face, hardly recognising him. It was like seeing his face through a cracked mirror. He wasn't the handsome dad she knew. Suddenly in the silence her mother very loudly roared *'I hope you die, you bastard!'*

grabbing Georgia's hand and walking out into the bright daylight. Georgia was numbed and shocked at what had just occurred. What is happening? Was she going mad?

The police had been called to the scene of the accident and an officer was sent to the shop to deliver the news to her mother that day. And it's here that Tom could have easily got away with hiding the affair he'd been having if it hadn't been for the duty-bound police officer who added a minor detail about the accident, reciting from his notebook, '*He was holding a bunch of flowers while crossing the road*' and proceeded to describe exactly where the accident happened. Oh dear. Her mother knew where her (now ex) best friend lived. Oops. Funny how a few words can very quickly change relationships.

Aunt Mary was doing a pretty good cover up job, making sure Georgia didn't find out exactly what had occurred. It was only weeks afterwards that she discovered that her mother, Sylvie, had attempted suicide by taking an overdose after hearing the news. She was in the Bethnal Green Hospital, just yards from her mother's friend's house, while her husband, Georgia's father Tom, was in the other hospital. Everyone was just a mile or so away from each other and Georgia guessed visiting either of them would have been pretty problematic for all of them, including her mother's ex friend. Georgia knew her place and could understand her aunt not wanting her to get in the way at the time. She would have appreciated knowing what the hell was going on though.

Back to the box and the following in italics is the original manuscript which Georgia wrote all those years ago as a record of events that took place. She thought the book had come to a natural end then, not knowing it was AFTER this that her life was really going to change beyond her wildest imagination.

## CHAPTER THREE

# JOINING THE OLD AND NEW

*As far back as she could remember Georgia thought she was nothing special. She had a regular mum and dad and was an 'only child.' She did always think it was an odd description of her and had a strange feeling that something had, somehow, gone wrong with the mixture and that's why they never risked having another child. After all, her mother often used to remind her "If you don't behave yourself, I'll take you back to where I got you and get the little boy in the next bed instead". Georgia assumed her mother would rather swop her than risk having another one.*

*She was a friendly and outgoing child, gregarious even, and knew it was very important to please her mother. She wanted her to be proud of her and was always polite and courteous to everyone. "I can take her anywhere," Sylvie would announce to complete strangers and Georgia was happy to do what she was told, however odd she thought it was. She was like any other child who loved and trusted their parents, even though her father only seemed around to tuck her in at night as he was always home late from work.*

*Tom had a small factory in Dalston, East London. He was a master tailor and employed half a dozen or so machinist making high quality ladies coats for big fashion houses in the West End. Sylvie was a seamstress and worked with him occasionally although, one year when Georgia was 11, Sylvie decided, by her own volition, to buy an old glass-blowers factory near Well Street market and within a couple of months, had it converted into a retail dress shop, with a two-bedroomed flat behind, a small garden and rear access to a side road. Tom always seemed to be at the factory and Georgia was often by herself, playing alone in the closed shop after school. Her mother appeared to be making all the decisions about their new home, directing builders and tradesmen, putting up stud walls, installing a handmade open-treaded staircase made by the new neighbour, a traditional carpenter who owned the empty shop next door. Lots of work, noise and mess. Georgia found the special place all to herself in the evening when the shop was closed. Just by sliding the door between the shop and flat, she could pretend it was her space. She often played by herself, imagining she was a teacher with her blackboard and chalk and then run and sit by the shop counter pretending to be the pupil. Unbeknown to her, the move to their new home was to mean their lives were never going to be the same again.*

*There were many changes for Georgia that year. She had passed her 11 plus exam and assumed she would be going to the same secondary school as her friends, but Sylvie was set on her attending a well-respected grammar school in North London where she did get along nicely enough for a few years. That was until the day she came home to find her aunt waiting for her and her father's road accident.*

*Georgia had been duly delivered back home after what seemed like months and guessed now her mother felt stronger and able to deal with life again. It seemed an age before Tom was discharged from the hospital and he came home looking tired and thin. Sylvie told Georgia how he had to have a special diet to build him up again. "Good" thinking it a positive move for them and prayed they'd be able to forget the past and be happy together again soon.*

*Although Tom had always busied himself with his work, he was now more remote than ever as the arguments between the couple grew and one afternoon on her way home from school, walking through the back door Georgia heard her mother shouting and, as she peered through the side window, she saw Tom sitting on one of the open stair treads halfway up the staircase sobbing like a child. She could see Sylvie standing over him, shouting. Georgia didn't know (and didn't want to know) what she was saying. All she knew was, it was something terrible and it was like watching a silent film, except she couldn't bear to watch. Still in her school uniform, she left her school bag outside the back door, grabbed her bike and headed for the local park and arriving at the boating pond, stood by the statue of the dog that had saved someone's life by rescuing them in the water years earlier.*

*Uncertain how long to stay out for, eventually she came home as it was getting dark to find Tom and his car had gone. Sylvie was silent and behaved like nothing had happened. As young as she was, it was obvious now that Georgia knew their relationship had deteriorated. It was clear Tom couldn't give up his mistress and she knew he had left now to be with her.*

*So Sylvie had survived the overdose and Tom had gone to live with Rita, the now ex-best friend of her mother in what Georgia assumed was the life he wanted, happily ever after. Without her.*

'We're getting divorced' Sylvie had announced with great gusto one Saturday morning, her stern eyes making it quite clear that the subject was not open for discussion. Georgia's whole life had just crumbled and nothing was clear anymore. And she couldn't express her feelings about any of it either because she wasn't allowed to broach the subject with her mother. In fact, there were very few subjects she was allowed to speak about. "Do as I say, not what I do" was her mother's favourite motto. Perhaps that's why, one rainy afternoon in her bedroom Georgia started writing about the situation she was living with. Writing her own account of the trauma she was going through, she gave it the title "The Other Woman" and secretly kept the handwritten notes in an old black ring-binder under her bed.

After writing just a few pages, her mother stormed into her room one evening with those angry piercing eyes she was well-practised at using, silently pulling the binder from Georgia's hands, tearing out the pages and ripping them up in front of her. Georgia saw her point of view immediately. The title must have been a bit insensitive. She was always able to justify her mother's actions. After all, she was the one going through the trauma, not Georgia. There was no reason for her to dwell on it. It was nothing to do with her anyway according to Sylvia. How stupid of her to try to write a book. The notes were not spoken or thought of again until now. She was living in a world of adults and was not allowed in. She was kept separate. Her mother spoke with just a look and she knew her place.

*But before the divorce was official, her school work was, just like Georgia was feeling, non-existent. She had been warned by the school Head that she would be kept back a year unless she started concentrating more. But she didn't care about school or anything else. Her senses were numb.*

*And it was around that time of the divorce that Georgia became aware of the peculiar jerking sensations in her arms and legs. For no apparent reason, her hand would twitch uncontrollably. Or one leg would just kick out, landing her on the floor completely dazed and puzzled. She remembers one day getting dressed and had just pulled out the bottom drawer of her dressing table when her legs were thrown up into the air as if by magic. Her back landed straight onto the corner of the dresser and felt it stab her back sharply. It was so painful she cried out. Her mother calling up "What have you done?." When she explained what had happened, as usual, she replied, "Don't be so silly, you're imagining things."*

*A week or so later she was running a bath when, as she leaned over to feel the temperature of the water, her legs jerked again and she fell directly onto the mixer taps, crushing one of her (already tender from 'growing pains' Sylvie had said) breasts. She remembers very well the bruise that turned from blue to yellow and stayed yellow for months to come. Everything was "growing pains" in her mother's eyes but never knowing if, how, when or where the next twitch would happen, Georgia became terribly self-conscious. At 15 she was now dating but had to keep her distance physically, not knowing when the next twitch was going to happen or how severe it was going to be.*

*Over the next few months, her limbs were twitching more and more and desperate to find out what was happening to her, she only knew one person to turn to and she was not helping at all. There was no Google in those days and she didn't want to trouble Tom. It was no surprise when her mother rejected her utterances yet again, this time considering the situation a little, "You're a hypochondriac. You're imagining all of this. Don't be so ridiculous. It's nothing."*

*After several months of twitching, jerking and feeling like a complete idiot, "Nothing" turned into epilepsy. Georgia hadn't seen her father for some months when he appeared quite suddenly at her bedside alone in the hospital one afternoon. It was obvious that he was extremely uncomfortable, embarrassed even, about her being epileptic and suggested quietly that it was best she didn't tell anyone about it. Her mother on the other hand had earlier insisted that she tell absolutely everyone that she came into contact with and that Georgia should explain to them what to do in the event of a fit, always volunteering to any stranger that cared to listen that her daughter was epileptic and the procedures to follow when confronted with an epileptic. Ah Mum knows best.*

*The consultant neurologist prescribed medication that controlled the fits and she came home feeling terribly embarrassed at the thought of going to the market place again but after a few weeks she summoned up the courage to see her friends and was delighted at their welcome and concern. They showered her with genuine care and kindness. There had been no reason to feel awkward with any of the stallholders. They were great. They cared.*

*After the divorce, school became a pointless exercise for Georgia. There was no reason to stay if she could leave. She needed a change and enrolled in the local secretarial college. It was a huge place with hundreds of students. It was easy to blend into the background and do hardly anything, although she did discover Judo and metalwork classes. One occasion in a Judo session she was winded during a body drop by a larger girl than herself. Georgia was thin and puny and tough she wasn't, but she did make a fabulous bracelet made of brass in her metalwork class and was thrilled with it too.*

*She had only been at college a few months and managed to get a Saturday job in a dress shop around the corner from Tom's factory. Against her mother's warnings, Georgia always made a point of finding him on a Saturday, sometimes for lunch if he wasn't too busy. She knew he was in one of three places, the factory, the betting shop, or the car auction, just around the corner. Sometimes she knew he was busy and would just pop in to say hello. He was still her dad. She loved him and she missed him and called him on the phone whenever she could. He however, never called her or came to see her at home or invited her to his new home with Rita .*

*Georgia had regular friends outside college, although she always felt like an outsider even though she couldn't pinpoint the exact reason why. She'd made friends at college too and one of the girls was a real trend-setter, always wearing original creations never seen in the shops. One day she wore a jumper that Georgia instantly fell in love with and asked if she could buy it. The new friend agreed and the next day she came home thrilled to be wearing this skin-tight, brown and cream Fair isle sweater. It had been shrunk to perfection and she loved squeezing herself into it. What a great fashion statement in the early 70's.*

*But when she got home, her mother took an instant dislike to it and said so at every given moment. Wearing it one evening while she was watching TV, sitting crouched on a footstool, Sylvie, with no word of warning crept up behind her with pair of tailor's shears and cut the back of the jumper from the bottom all the way to the top. Georgia was shocked and jumped a little when she felt the cold steel on her back but, as usual, Georgia justified her mother's actions. 'She doesn't like this on me" and within seconds, she let it pass. Well, she must be right. She must have looked silly in it. She had completely destroyed it and there was no hope of ever wearing it again anyway.*

*There were many occasions when Georgia asked her mother why this or that and, as always, she was reduced to an insignificant noise or was just ridiculed for being so stupid. On some occasions, her mother didn't even bother to answer her questions and just dismissed her with a huff. She learnt fast never to show any emotion. It was of no importance. What she felt was of no consequence to Sylvie.*

*There was the occasion when her mother became very good friends with Tom's mistress Rita not long after the divorce. Georgia couldn't bear to see them together, like nothing had ever happened. Her mother had told her ages ago what a tramp and marriage-breaker this 'hussy' was. How could she befriend her? She cringed whenever she saw them together. They seemed really close. How could they be? She must be missing something that others knew. Maybe she was just plain stupid.*

*As she grew older, her mother became more and more hostile towards Georgia. Feelings were dismissed almost automatically. Whatever was said, howsoever important it was to her that she said something, was always without exception ridiculed. "You don't know what you're talking about" or "You're lying" or "Don't be so ridiculous, you're mad."*

*She knew her mother didn't believe a word she said which made her doubt every thought she had, but what did she do or say that was so wrong? She was too afraid to ask. Attempting to speak with her mother was futile. Sylvie had no interest in what she had to say and so she just lived accordingly. After all, there was no point in having an opinion about anything when it was never acknowledged. She knew her mother must be right because she knew better than her. She was her mother, and all mums know best, don't they?*

*But living at home was not good. Georgia was sixteen when Sylvie received the decree-nisi in the post, singing happily out loud, which annoyed Georgia no end. Along with the end of the marriage came a new kind of mother. Now that her father was no longer living with them she made it quite clear that Georgia would be taking a back seat in her life. "You're a big girl now. You don't' need to be around me anymore." She seemed so ruthless. She noticed how her mother let nothing stand in her way. Out most nights, staying out late, often coming home with a man, Georgia in her bedroom, would hear them climbing the stairs, laughing. She'd take him to her bedroom, which was next to hers, and that was all she was really sure of. She had no idea what caused the strange noises that came from her mother's room and could only imagine terrible reasons why she could hear knocking, banging and moaning. If he was hurting her mother, could Georgia save her? And was she going to be next? She was so afraid. All she could do was hide under the bedcovers and hope the noises would stop and pray he would soon be gone.*

*He was usually gone by the morning but she was afraid for their safety during those nights, scared to sleep until she knew it was safe. Knowing she couldn't discuss such things with her mother only confirmed what she already knew. It was none of her business. She used to catch up with sleep at weekends, sometimes not surfacing until 2pm or 3pm. She was a teenager so that kind of behaviour was expected of her anyway she guessed.*

*Georgia began staying out late too even though her friends were making their way home from the West End clubs before the last train, she would purposely miss it so she could get home much later. Often, rather than listen to those noises, she'd wait for Samantha's or Le Kilt, to close around 3am and then walk up to Holborn tube station which was always closed by then. Sitting alone outside on the pavement, she would wait for the metal gates to be opened at 5am. Catching the first train of the morning was usually a good bet. Hopefully her mother would be alone by the time she got home.*

*The 70's was a great time to be a teenager. The atmosphere in the West End was fantastic. There were so many people enjoying this special time but Georgia always felt like an outsider, avoiding one on one conversations with boys, even though she was now shapely and quite attractive. It was beginning to dawn on her that the noises she was hearing at home were to do with sex. She knew she had been disturbed by it and knew by association to keep her distance where boys were concerned. She was seventeen and boys were showing an interest in her but she wasn't ready for a boyfriend.*

*A couple of the boys in her crowd of friends gave her the nickname "Elliott Ness." They were right. She was untouchable and there was nothing she could do about it. There was no one to confide in. She had to keep the thoughts to herself. Her girlfriends were kind but she felt it was impossible to discuss such a subject with them or anyone.*

*There seemed to be a lot of changes going on around her then, including her relationship with her mother, which was now growing more distant than ever. Convinced (conditioned by her mother) that her father was of no real use to her other than for the two pounds pocket money he gave her if and when she saw him. Her mother's opinion of him was so very low and she was persistently reminding Georgia of his mistakes and failings. Whatever was happening in the adult world was not her place to* question and she certainly couldn't speak up to defend him. That would be disloyal to her mother. It would be pointless anyway. Now Tom had a new life with this other woman and Georgia wasn't meant to be a part of it. That scene of him sobbing on the stairs still haunted her. What had her mother said that day that had made him so upset?

Sylvie was becoming more complex than ever. Now in her forties, she was a very attractive woman with a good figure, raven black hair and full lips "I look like Ava Gardner" she often used to say.

Sylvie had recently learned to drive and one day, on her way home from her sister's house she was telling Georgia she'd "seen a man in a pink shirt waiting for a bus and stopped to give him a lift. I love men in pink shirts. It makes them look really sexy." she said.

His name was John and Sylvie introduced him as "daddy," laughing as she said it. It sickened Georgia. Even though she hardly saw Tom these days, he was still her father and how could she be so insensitive. John was far less offensive and seemed to take a genuine interest in her and her school work but her mother put a halt to conversation of any depth between them. It was made clear that she 'was not to get close to him or any of the men she chose to date.'

By now her mother was making blatant sexual advances towards men in general and Georgia found it more and more distressing. The public exhibition of her mother's physical desires was a significant obstacle in Georgia's own sexual development. No surprise there.

## CHAPTER FOUR

# HELLO ADULT WORLD

After leaving college Georgia went into her first job as an office junior in a menswear company just a few minutes' walk from home. One of the girls in the office was epileptic and after witnessing her regular fits, Georgia realised how lucky she was to have had just the one in the marketplace. But she was easily bored as a filing clerk and lunchtime telephonist and decided to find something more exciting in the West End. The next job was to be a training ground for every job that followed.

Now she was a receptionist/telephonist in a record company in Dean Street, Soho. Specialists in classical music with a retail shop on the ground floor and offices upstairs, this was a real job. She loved music and in 1971 Soho was a great place to be, only minutes from the clubs she already knew and there was Carnaby Street, just a few streets away as it was becoming the centre of everyone's world. There was a cosmopolitan atmosphere. There was Ronnie Scott's, Berwick Street Market, record studios, Chubby's Deli, the first Pizza Express to open in London right next to the shop and Liberty's and Regent Street and Oxford Street. There was lunch on the grass in Soho Square, hippies and punks, jazz record shops, coffee bars and all kinds of weird and wonderful things on her doorstep and she was in the centre of it all. She'd meet up with her friends after work and after a bite to eat would all head for the Bataclan, Le Kilt, Samantha's, Rasputin's, Birdland, Countdown, Anthea's, Les Enfants Terrible or La Val Bonne, but she always took a step back, desperately wanting to be a part of it but never wanting any real attention.

Within a year, Georgia had been promoted to assistant manager and felt she belonged more to a family than a company. She knew the record business well by now having been given hands-on education in classical music by most of the staff. In the mornings she would walk into the shop to say hello to the guys before climbing the stairs to the office, and sometimes Neville, the senior 'gay' would skip and waltz towards her as Strauss played on the loudspeaker. Their arms would fling around each other as they met in the centre of the shop, falling about laughing. They were such happy days at work and as her confidence grew daily, one morning on her way into work she realised the shop's large window was empty and unused and mentioned to her boss that the window could be put to good use and suggested displaying some record sleeves there. He agreed and suggested she go to evening classes to learn window dressing. The College for Distributive Trades was just around the corner in Charing Cross Road. Perfect.

The college was opposite Centrepoint by Tottenham Court Road Station and once a week she would go to the evening classes at 7pm on Fridays after work and come home on the No.6 bus around 10pm. There were lots of new people at this college. It was as if the whole of London came alive inside and outside the college and being an observer was fantastic.

Georgia was learning how to make huge crepe paper flowers during one class. She had the scissors in her hand when a strange feeling came over her. Something told her to put them down and the next thing she remembered was being carried out of the college on a stretcher in front of what seemed like the entire world. It was only when she was in the ambulance that she discovered she had had a fit and was being taken to Charing Cross Hospital. The doctor there told her to "Rest a while, then you can go home." She waited few minutes after he left and then climbed out of the bed, finding her way to the exit and into the night of the West End.

As she left the building she saw a public telephone and called Tom (there were no mobile phones in those days), not certain why but just to let him know what had happened. She knew her mother wouldn't be home and didn't even try calling her. Tom sounded genuinely concerned. He told her to stay where she was and he would pick her up, but she was getting a bus just outside the hospital that would take her all the way home. She had had enough fuss made of her for one evening and she didn't want to impose on his privacy, still feeling the need to protect her mother from him anyway. After all, Georgia might appear disloyal if Sylvie saw her with him. The bus journey took about an hour and, not bothering to even put the lights on downstairs when she got home, put herself to bed.

Unlike the first fit, this one was different. Georgia was more self-conscious than ever and felt sick at the thought of going back to the evening classes. She knew she couldn't. That was just too much to bear and she never did finish the course or learn how to make the big crepe flowers.

She was always looking for an escape from life at home and wanting to learn whatever she could when she could and often joined local evening classes, including studying

Calligraphy, a real passion of hers, where she was told in no uncertain terms that her 'A's were not correct." She spent that first lesson writing over a hundred lines of lower-case 'a's to satisfy the tutor. She never went back after that first class, even though she needed to get away from home. She never forgot the experience either, which was to be to her advantage some forty years later, when she decided to share the things she had taught herself about handwriting. Unbeknown to her then, Calligraphy and Graphology was to become a significant part of her life and would owe much to it as it gave her the inner strength to carry on despite times of great adversity ahead.

Two years later, she was still working for the music company and was chatting with her boss about his daughter who lived in Athens with her Greek husband. Their neighbour was looking for an English Nanny to look after their two small children. Did she know of anyone? She said she'd ask some friends if anyone would be interested.

When she came home from work that night, Sylvie was sitting at the dining table with another 'new' friend, tucking into a meal. "Make yourself something in the kitchen" she said as Georgia looked at their plates of food. She knew she was in the way and headed for the kitchen making a sandwich and quickly taking herself upstairs to her room. She got to thinking about the family in Greece looking for a Nanny and wondered if she might fit the bill. She was so unhappy and just wanted to get away. She needed to make big changes to her life.

## CHAPTER FIVE

# EFF HARISTO

*The next day she thought she should talk the idea of Greece over with her mother and picked what she thought was a good time to speak to her. She had only just started to describe the job when she was interrupted "Sure, you're a big girl now, go!" and Sylvie showed no further interest in the subject. Georgia was nineteen now and what Sylvie had said made sense so she made the arrangements and in a matter of weeks was travelling by car with her boss's son-in-law Costas, to Athens. She would have loved to share the driving but she wasn't allowed to drive for another three years and only then if there were no more fits. They drove through London, Paris, Lyon into Italy, seeing many wonderful sights. Brindisi was the most memorable for Georgia. True Italy with picturesque countryside and the clearest water in a stream she had ever seen. They enjoyed a genuine Italian pizza there while they waited for the ferry to take them to Piraeus.*

*The journey from London to Athens had taken 5 days, staying in pensions and motels when Costas was too tired to drive through the night. It was regrettable that he had to do all the driving but it was a great relief to her that Costas had been a thorough gentleman throughout the journey. Georgia had learned over the years to be ready to submit when a man was interested in her and was thankful that she didn't have to experience such things on this occasion. She had learned all about that from her mother's encounters with men.*

*They arrived in Athens in May 1973 and her new family consisted of Maria, wife of Nikos and their two beautiful daughters, Natasha was five and Martha was two. Nikos was a civil engineer with his own company in Athens.*

He told her about their summer apartment in Kalamata, a coastal resort popular with the natives, where they would all be spending the summer together, in a couple of months.

Nikos had been involved in the building of the apartment in Kalamata and the block had been named after him. At both homes there were only two bedrooms so she shared a room with the children and worked hard. She enjoyed being with the children 24/7 and although her pay was only bed, board and cash equivalent to £10 a week, she loved being part of this family. They all made her feel so wanted. She was so well cared for and before she knew it she had broken through the language barrier, giving her a taste of the real Greece most tourists miss.

It took ten months before the soaring temperatures and the Greek cigarettes took their toll on Georgia. She had developed a bad cough which was getting worse and being unfamiliar with Greek pharmacies, it wasn't easy finding a remedy. It was only after speaking with Tom on the phone (she often called him at the factory) that she decided it was time to come home. He seemed concerned and wired her £50 for her flight home. She called her mother to tell her she was on her way home and to her surprise she said she'd pick her up at the airport.

Saying her goodbyes to everyone she had grown to love in Greece, she left with every hope of one day returning to see how the children were growing.

At Gatwick she spotted her mother and walked towards her and it wasn't until she spoke that Sylvie realised it was *her daughter standing in front of her. Georgia had always been painfully thin but one of her greatest pleasures in Greece apart from her new family there, had been the food. It was no wonder she didn't recognise her. Her nearly orange hair had now turned white, bleached by the sun and she was at least two stone heavier than when she'd left, a year earlier. It would not be long before she went back to her near anorexic state again.*

*In the car Sylvie seemed to pay little attention to Georgia's chatter about Greece and quickly turned the subject to her own news. Sylvie had met a man and they were getting married. "You'll meet him soon," she went on "He lives in Newcastle (some 400 miles away from London) and he's asked me to move up there with him". "What about me?" Georgia asked. "Oh you can live up there too if you want, or you can stay here, behind the shop. I'll probably rent that part too. Get a couple of flatmates to help pay the rent. I'm thinking of selling the whole freehold to Neil, but I'm not sure yet." Neil, another friend of her mothers.*

*It was two weeks later that Sylvie told Georgia in passing that her she had discovered the guy from Newcastle was already married with two kids. Georgia presumed she would get over it soon. All her relationships didn't seem to last very long but apparently this one was different. She said she loved him too much to give him up and within a couple of weeks she'd bought a mobile home near Whitley Bay and was gone.*

*Months after coming back from Greece Georgia's cough was getting worse. At times she had trouble catching her breath. Her GP had referred her to the London Chest*

*Hospital in Bethnal Green and was now sitting in the waiting room for over an hour before being called in to see the consultant. He took some x-rays and told her to wait outside again. After another long wait she was called in again and the very quiet, serious doctor said 'Did you see all those people out there in the waiting room' she nodded. 'Well, I have to tell five of them today they've got lung cancer. You haven't, but if you don't give up the cigarettes, I might see you again and you may not be so lucky next time.'*

*But Georgia didn't care about living or dying. Why did she even bother this doctor? He had much more important patients than her. Dying was never a conscious option but if it happened, at least she wouldn't inflict herself on others. The world would be a better place without her in it. No one would miss her. She had created this life of hers and she didn't deserve any better. Well, just look how her mother treated her. If she didn't think she was worth anything, then that is how it's supposed to be. It must be so.*

## CHAPTER SIX

# HOORAY FOR DAD

Back in England work was easy to find and Georgia had diversified into recruiting foreign medical students as nurses for the Eastern Hospital back in Homerton. She was promoted to an HCO, Higher Clerical Officer where, among her usual admin duties, she created the hospital magazine, editing, producing and printing every issue for all the staff on the Gestetner stencil duplicator in her own private office. She produced articles, crosswords and puzzles and her passion for calligraphy was stimulated by the elegant copperplate writing on an envelope which contained an entry for the magazine cover competition. She contacted the writer who was to design the front cover for 'The Eastern.' He was a calligraphy teacher and gave her private lessons at her request. Wow.

Georgia was twenty when her provisional driving licence arrived in the post. She had almost forgotten about it, resigning herself to public transport for the foreseeable future. She didn't think she was special enough for a licence like her friends had. Then she realised she was going to be just like them, as soon as she could pass the test.

Only by her own attempts it seemed, she was still in touch with Tom and would still call in to see him at the factory from time to time. She showed him her new provisional licence and he said he'd help find her a car once she had passed the test. He was mechanically minded and knew a lot about cars. He'd taken her a few times to the local car auctions and as far as she knew, he never actually bought a vehicle from there but simply enjoyed the atmosphere and company of other car enthusiasts.

*She actually knew so little about him. She had so little time with him. He had been working so hard before he left. Georgia was only able to see him when she visited the factory. Sometimes he'd come up with neat ideas and inventions. He once made a shower out of a washing machine by constructing a curtain rail over a shower tray and adjusting the cycle of the old washing machine, connecting a pipe to the water outlet to run the water back into the washing machine. It did mean showering with dirty water all the time, but Georgia thought it was great fun. Her dad was so clever. His skills at tailoring never ceased to amaze her. The dexterity with which he applied himself to every aspect of tailoring was an art in itself. She had watched him when she was small, use every machine in the factory as well as designing dress and coat patterns, cutting 50 layers of cloth at the same time. She had seen him use all kinds of stitching by hand and machine, as well as using a steam iron with a block of wood to cool the cloth quickly like he'd done it all his life. He was artistic too. He once drew the most beautiful white horse on a spare piece of grey cloth using just tailor's chalk and she never forgot how quickly he drew it. As a toddler, she had played hide and seek under the huge cutting table amongst the long rolls of cloth but still, she knew little about him. About his opinions or dreams or anything. She knew it wasn't her place to ask. She **never** asked questions.*

*Georgia knew so little about him. She remembered after they'd moved to the shop and he'd had his piano delivered. She knew he loved jazz and was a good pianist. Oscar Peterson, Duke Ellington, Ella, Sinatra and Gershwin were familiar sounds to her. Rhapsody In Blue still makes her cry today. In those early days of the shop, Friday nights became 'jazz night' when Tom's friends would start pouring in with their instruments. The whole place used to shake with the sound of the trumpets, drums, sax, trombone and the piano. In the centre of the row of shops only used in the daytime meant making loud noises in the evening was not a problem. There was always a piano at home and Georgia had learned to play by ear and would often 'jam' with Tom or her grandfather, but this was dad's time and she would go to her room to do her homework and her mother would go out for the evening. She had no idea where she went.*

*Georgia's memory of her father contained little snippets, like him buying her an electric xylophone and showing her how to play it, just behind the shop window when the blinds were down. And him going through her maths homework with her in his factory. She recalled the fish tank balanced precariously on the top of the tv. The inside was so dirty, it was hard to see anything in the water and she used to stare for ages before catching a fleeting glimpse of the one massive goldfish. Times must have been hard for him after the divorce. Her mother told her 'He's no good to you' and 'you don't need him' and not wanting to go against her, she believed her mother and tried to keep her distance. But she soon started to miss him, taking the bus to Dalston Junction most weekends Tom loved cars and he'd often be seen with a different car every week. Georgia liked the one that ran sparks along the dashboard when he put the two wires together to get it started. Ignition keys? Nah, not necessary with her dad. He also had a handy knack of running out of petrol just as he was heading downhill with a petrol station at the bottom. She noticed how he recently added a camp bed in the tiny office space in the factory and realised this was where he had to sleep after the divorce. He was proud of the shower he'd constructed and Georgia was so impressed with this new invention of his, but he must have spent a long time there on his own, which is why she assumed he needed to set up the bed. She had been kept away from all news about her parents but why didn't anyone tell her anything? And why didn't he keep in touch? Why didn't he call or ever ask to see her? And why did she only see him when she went looking for him? Why couldn't she ask questions?*

*Twelve professional driving lessons and the last one was on the way to the test centre. Not daring to believe she could actually pass, she ran to find her instructor after the test to tell him. 'I've passed! I've passed! First time!' It was real. She had been handed the pass paper. It was official.*

*She didn't know it but Tom had bought a car and it was waiting for her. He'd kept it in a side street near the factory and she felt odd getting into it for the first time. It was a small white Vauxhall Viva and it was wonderful "Thank you Dad!" She realised she was free. After the longing to drive for so many years, her passion for driving could begin now and how precious that passion was. Total independence. It hadn't crossed her mind until she got home… why couldn't he bring the car around to where she lived? And why did he never call her?*

*The shop was now empty and as per her mother's instructions, she advertised for a flatmate and took on the first friendly face that applied. The girl was slow, mainly in the rent department, as well as being extremely accident prone with her mother's crockery and ornaments. After a month, she had to go. The second one was a beautiful Penthouse Pet. Georgia watched as cars curb-crawled alongside this ravishing beauty without fail whenever she stepped outside the shop. Housework was not part of this girl's routine and she complained constantly about everything being messy and how "I don't do chores." Georgia found herself resenting the piles of washing up she left for her every night and it wasn't long before she was gone and the traffic moved at a regular pace once again.*

*She rang her mother in Newcastle, saying she couldn't find a suitable flatmate. "Right!" she said, "I'm selling. It'll take some time for it to go through, but I should be able to finalise everything in about six months".*

*Georgia was 21 and had left the Eastern Hospital to work as a permanent temp for a large employment agency in the City. The assignments were varied, perfect for her at the time. Insurance clerk, legal sec, medical sec, a fashion office, even Diners Club switchboard operator at Oxford Circus. She enjoyed this variety. Being a temp taught her how to adapt, which suited her. She couldn't stand the thought of every day being the same. It meant being flexible and she was frequently offered permanent jobs during these assignments. Maybe something she liked would eventually come her way.*

On the train home one evening reading the *Evening Standard* she noticed a job vacancy she couldn't ignore. *'Hotel receptionist/telephonist required with accommodation. Five Star Hotel in the Isle of Wight.'* She called the number. A lady asked for her details and after just a few minutes talking, she said *'You've got the job!'*

*'What? Without an interview?'*

*'Yes'"* she said *'but you'll have to be here in two weeks' time.'*

She was ready to go right there and then but waited patiently, planning the days ahead as she registered her car for the island and booked the ferry. Then she was off, not believing her luck in landing such a great post at the height of the season, and just when she needed to make a new start too. Pointing her lovely car in the direction of Portsmouth, she drove without stopping, passing the Devil's Punchbowl and glorious countryside with lush fields, and the ferry, travelling to an island all by herself. This was exciting. She felt alive.

But she wasn't so happy after arriving at the Grand Hotel. It was an impressive building at the end of the promenade. She left her luggage in the boot of the car and as she walked up to Reception, was greeted by a waiter who had just come out of a side door. Explaining why she was there, he said nothing and with a smile gestured her to follow him. He took her through the dining room, then the kitchen and then out into some kind of back yard and pointed. "This is your quarters" he said as she hesitantly moved closer to a broken wooden door with large holes. It *was more like a shed than a room. She knew she felt low about herself but there was no way she could stay there. "I wouldn't let a dog sleep in this place. Is this a joke?" she asked. "No, this is our in-house accommodation" he replied with an unconvincing smile.*

*As she came back into the main lobby, there was a chambermaid answering the phones behind the reception desk, more waiters carrying luggage and stopping to ask questions, they complained they hadn't been paid for weeks. It was a bad version of Fawlty Towers and she decided to leave. But where to now? She was on an island with no job, nowhere to stay and it was the start of the summer season.*

*She got back in the car and eventually found the unemployment office, where they looked at her as some kind of oddball, saying "Sorry, we can't help you as you are not a resident on the island." She got back in the car and headed for the ferry and as she drove along the promenade she passed a small "STAFF WANTED" sign in a little wooden booth on the beach. She stopped the car and got out. "What could staff do on the beach?" she wondered. The man behind the counter of the kiosk was the owner who explained it was an easy job. All she had to do was walk along the beach and take photos of holiday makers. "Then give them a receipt and they collect their photo in a souvenir frame the following day." He had a small studio in the High Street where he developed the pictures. He told her he lived somewhere she didn't know on the island with his wife and children and as she explained her situation, he laughed, as if he knew how bad the hotel she had just left was and said she could* start straight away if she wanted to. He said she could stay at the studio if she wished until she found somewhere permanent to live. Georgia and her car followed his to the studio where she was greeted by what must have been the largest Irish Wolfhound in the world. It was a small space but big enough to wash and sleep in. He gave her a key and went back to his kiosk, taking the dog with him. She washed, changed into her swimwear topped with a t shirt and jeans and went back to the beach to start her new career as a beach photographer.

Quite by accident she had found a fantastic job. Just wearing a bikini and the expensive Cannon camera supplied by the boss around her neck, she spent three summer months taking pictures of people on the beach. The weather was hot and she quickly made friends. In fact one of the deeply tanned and handsome deckchair attendants seemed extremely friendly and very quickly, they were dating.

Michael was a little shy whenever they were out together but she liked that quietness about him. They had a good time together. He didn't have a car so Georgia did all the driving. He was an islander and helped her find a flat to rent in Shanklin, just a couple of miles from the photo booth.

They'd been seeing each other for about a month when one day a new girl started work on the beach and Georgia was asked to show her the ropes. As she walked along the promenade she saw Michael and waved. "I know Michael" the new girl said. "Oh, how's that?" Georgia asked. "He's in my brother's class at school." What?

*Georgia had been going out with a 15-year-old boy? She was twenty-one. His bronzed body, handsome face and shyness had hidden much more than she realised. How stupid and embarrassed was she? There goes another job she had to quit. It was too awkward to stay. Mike didn't seem bothered and appeared to find the new girl more interesting now anyway.*

*By now she had found a small studio to rent where her and Mike had spent some evenings together. It was a dark and damp room with a bathroom along the hall but she was free, away from her mother and quickly found another job as a barmaid in the Theatre Bar on the Pier. It was a very posh affair and she will never forget what happened to her there. Despite the doctor's warning, she was still smoking and one evening intended to buy some cigarettes while at work. In this bar, the cash from cigarette sales were kept in a beer mug, away from the two tills used for the drinks. It was just before the show interval and needing change from a £5 note, Georgia put a five-pound note in the drinks mug and took out the £5 in change. She then put the correct money in the beer mug, pouring the rest, quite legitimately, into her purse. As the bar began to fill with visitors she turned to serve the first customer and the manager's face was right in front of her. "Out!" he shouted, in front of everyone in the now packed bar. "Get out!" Yelling at the top of his voice, getting louder and louder. "But…." she tried to continue but he shouted over her "Out! Out!." Each time she tried to explain what he had obviously misread, he simply shouted louder and stronger. Every plea she made for him to listen to her was drowned out by his voice. She felt like she was dumb, like no real sound was coming out of her mouth. He was telling her to get out like a common thief, thinking she had stolen from the till. But she hadn't. She must have tried to speak for at least 5 minutes to make him listen but he was more forceful than she was and starting to cry, she just ran, probably just like he expected her to, maybe just like a real thief would do. She knew he would find all the monies in order at the end of that evening but he wouldn't let her explain and had condemned her for a crime she hadn't committed. There was absolutely nothing she could do about it. No one wanted to hear what she had to say. She'd been on the island some six months and now she wanted to go home.*

*But where was home? Was it where it used to be now?*

# CHAPTER SEVEN

# MOVING ON
# AND OUT

Georgia came home to find her mother busying herself loading boxes in the shop. She had sold up and was arranging herself and her mobile home, having it transported from Newcastle to Braintree, a little nearer to home. Why? She didn't know and didn't ask.

Sylvie gave her the date she had to be out by, but somehow Georgia just couldn't take seriously the fact that she was going to leave her to find her own place. She would have to move out soon and find somewhere to live.

Georgia's grandfather was always in the background. He was one of the kindest people she knew. He always had time for her even though her life had been pretty busy for a long time now. From the day she was born she knew he idolised her. He called her "the baby" and took her and her grandmother everywhere together. In fact, as she checked her memory, both he and her grandmother had brought her up most of the time when she was young. Well, Georgia's parents were very busy people.

Her grandmother had died when she was 11 and he lived not far from Tom's factory and she had always kept in touch with him, visiting whenever she could. When she told him what was happening at home, he didn't hesitate to offer sharing his one-bedroomed flat with her. In fact he insisted. She was grateful and moved in just days before the shop's sale was completed.

Georgia had met someone just a week before she moved in with Grandpa. She and some of her old friends had been out one evening at Rosetti's, a wine bar in St John's Wood when she struck up a conversation with a familiar *face at the bar. She'd dated a few guys since she got back from the Isle of Wight, nothing serious, nothing ever was with Georgia. It turned out that they'd done the 'scene' at the same time. The same discos, clubs and pubs and probably bumped into each other on many occasions. He was 5'5, stocky, not her usual type but he was funny, strong-minded and dependable. His name was Larry and he was a London cabbie.*

*Unusually, she invited him back to behind the shop just days before she was moving out. She had never brought a boyfriend back before and when she explained the situation he said there must be something fundamentally wrong with her mother. Georgia didn't understand what he meant and she certainly couldn't agree with him.*

*Larry helped her move her clothes into her grandfather's flat and as she started seeing a lot more of Larry, she soon found a little flat near her old school. The transition from her grandfather's to the studio flat was easy. Georgia had no furniture, in fact very little of anything but she had landed a job locally as a bus conductor for London Transport which, although this was shift work, she was earning exceptionally good money and discovered she loved working with the public. Suddenly, in her new place she felt surrounded by people who really cared about her. She had never known such attention before. It was nice and she liked it. Even her father came to visit and she made him dinner once. He said he enjoyed it and must have been very tactful considering Georgia was useless at cooking. It was to be the one and only meal she ever made for him.*

*Her place was perfect. Her own front door in a small purpose-built block made of red brick with its own private car park. She filled the place with furniture from Ikea and MFI. The sofa bed must have been one of the first in 1975. It was actually a single bed with throw-on cushions in the day and pillows at one end in the evening. How fab.*

*Larry was so caring and she wanted to be with him. She felt so protected and within a few months she asked him to move in with her. She may have had some ups and downs in the past, but she wanted to be part of a family and Larry had a mother, father, brother and sister. It was when they had been in the car on the way home from visiting Larry's parents that without any thought, as if by impulse, Georgia asked him if he would be the father of her children. Where the question came from she may never know but she remembered his reaction. He was just as stunned and surprised as she was for asking, and he thought about it for just a few moments and then said "Yes." She had never known a man to show such consideration and protectiveness for her. Larry was to become more important than she could have imagined in the years to come.*

*They decided to go and see Sylvie in Braintree to tell her the news. Georgia was speaking to her on a more regular basis now. Sylvie had told her about this marvellous site the static home was on. When they arrived, they entered a caravan park in a small field and Sylvie welcomed them with a wave and as they came in she began telling them about the new job she had, just across the road by the lake. She was in charge of preparing meals for the clubhouse attached to the lake which was used by water-skiers.*

Georgia had never enjoyed her mother's cooking and was always puzzled when she sang the praises of her own recipes. "Rather them than her" she thought.

Sylvie made a light lunch as Georgia and Larry started to explain their plans about setting a date for the engagement party and hopefully a wedding the following year. Georgia had never EVER discussed her mother's finances with her but the time had come to ask if she could help with the expense of a wedding. There was a lot of family to invite. Sylvie told them curtly she had £100 to give them and "that was it". Georgia felt ashamedly downhearted, hoping she had put aside a little more, especially after the sale of the property. Larry saw the disappointment in her eyes but, as usual, she never dared continue the conversation with her mother and felt like a spoilt brat as they drove home. What a cheek she had to expect anything. Larry said nothing but later told her he wasn't at all surprised at her mother's response.

Back home she called Tom and told him the news. He'd only met Larry once but seemed happy for them and said he'd let us know what he was going to give them for a wedding present. Georgia knew he was a heavy gambler and soon discovered that he had also not considered contributing anything to a wedding. Larry's parents gave them a lump sum of £1,000 and Georgia and Larry made the engagement party and wedding with that plus their own small amount of savings. Tom bought them a large fridge-freezer for their new home which they bought just before the wedding. Useful and practical. Perfect.

Larry and Georgia had just finished lunch one afternoon when the doorbell rang. It was her mother. She had only been to the flat once before and Georgia was very surprised to see her. She had come to make them an offer she didn't think they could refuse. Sylvie was going to make the engagement party at the clubhouse in Braintree. It was a lovely surprise but it wasn't practical plus the thought of her cooking, "Oh no" Georgia thought and tried to explain that both Larry's family and their family and friends all lived near to them. Sylvie was the only family member living so far way and they didn't think it was fair to expect everyone to travel so far, around 100 miles, for the party. She thought it was a wonderful gesture though but Sylvie would not take the hint and continued to rave over her cooking and completely ignored Georgia's diplomatic comments. Georgia tried to reason with her but she was so adamant she was right, that Larry's frustration began to show as he slammed his fist down on the table and started to shout at her. "Thank you but no thank you!" he yelled in her face.

Georgia had never seen an aggressive side of Larry before. What did it mean? She wasn't used to anyone shouting. She was confused and in a blind panic asked him to leave. He stormed out. "You're not going to marry a man like that are you?" her mother asked as he left. She said "I don't know." "Find someone else, you don't need anyone like that" her mother shrieked as she got up and said "Oh, by the way, your father has just had a son" as she closed the front door.

Suddenly after all the shouting Georgia was alone. A week later she was still alone and still confused. Larry had kept away and she was ready to resign herself to the single life again when the phone rang. It was a friend of Larry's parents, Sam. He had been told about the row with Larry and her mother and wanted Georgia to know something. She listened, finding it hard to believe that someone would take such trouble over a friend's son. He told her how he had known Larry and his family all of his life and how he knew Larry would never hurt her and was only full of love for her. Georgia was touched immensely by his dedication to help make things better between them and although she had no real reason to doubt her own belief in Larry, Georgia was fighting between him and her mother's opinion. She hadn't seen or spoken to him for some weeks because surely she should follow her mother's advice. Was it worth taking the risk? Marriage? It was a big step and she wasn't sure what love was and couldn't be sure she could ever know it. She certainly didn't ever want to go through her own divorce.

Even Larry's mother came to see her. She told Georgia how very upset he was and that he loved her very much. Georgia was still very unsure and asked Sylvie to speak to Larry's mother. After all, she valued her opinion, she knew she could help her decide the best thing to do. But Sylvie wouldn't hear of it. "It's got nothing to do with me and I don't want anything to do with the whole situation" she said. "It is none of my business and the decision is solely yours, Georgia" and Georgia decided to stick with Larry based on nothing but a blind faith that she would grow to love him in time.

# CHAPTER EIGHT

# WEDDING BELLES

As soon as she informed her mother of the date of the engagement party Sylvie became obstructive. First of all, she was not coming to the wedding unless she was sent her own personal invitation and then, a row broke out between Sylvie's sister and Georgia's mother-in-law-to-be. To this day, Georgia doesn't know what it was about. She did know that not one member of her family came to the engagement party, not even Tom, who she guessed was feeling a little awkward at the prospect of seeing his ex-wife's family after so long. Amongst friends, the only family that came were Larry's. They all seemed nice. The couple announced the wedding date for the following October.

Arrangements were made and they did the best they could with the budget. Georgia started looking at wedding dresses in magazines and thought it would be nice if her mother came with her to choose one. It could be a real bonding opportunity for them. It would be great. But Sylvie had no interest in such things. As usual, Georgia was disappointed but never questioned her about it. She asked Larry's mother and sister to come shopping instead, which they happily did although it was her mother she really wanted with her. She was feeling more depressed than ever.

Bride at Lord John in Wood Green had a sale on as she passed their window while shopping alone one day. She just grabbed a dress and veil off the rail, tried them on and said "I'll take these" to the assistant. The bridal department was upstairs and as she came down she noticed some white strappy shoes in the sale and tried *them on.  They seemed suitable, so she bought them.  There, all done.  What had she made such a fuss over?*

*Sylvie played no part whatsoever in the wedding preparations and only just managed to send her the addresses of long-lost aunts and uncles after constant pleading for months from Georgia.  She made no suggestions as to who should or shouldn't be invited and it took ages to persuade her to come to the actual wedding.  "If I'm not important enough for you to send an invitation to then I'm not coming!" Georgia posted her invitation and dismissed her attitude, again.  She had sent Tom an invitation too and she called him to see if he agreed he would be there to walk her down the aisle.  He had been so elusive and punctuality was never a strong point of his.  She just prayed he would actually turn up on the day.*

*The couple had bought a small semi-detached house just a month before the wedding and Georgia's mother had said she would be staying with her the night before.  Larry would be staying at his parents that night but how would it work with Sylvie being there when her father was supposed to be there too? She was too scared to ask.*

*Sylvie was watching TV the night before the wedding when Georgia thought she'd better go up and take the wedding dress and veil out of their boxes only to find the veil was badly creased.  She brought it down, plugged in the iron and unfolded the ironing board.  She was about to iron the veil when she froze.  What if she burnt it? She couldn't afford to make a mistake.  She'll ask her mother for her advice. 'Perhaps she would iron it for me.  She must have more experience about this kind of thing.' But*

*Sylvie refused. Simple as that. So Georgia gingerly ironed it and thankfully it remained intact.*

*She ran a bath for herself that evening and decided to have another one in the morning too. It was her wedding day and chattering away to Sylvie, mentioned she wanted to be the cleanest she could possibly be for this once in a lifetime occasion. Sylvie laughed and said "You're mad. I've never heard such rubbish."*

*The big day arrived. Georgia had had a perm (all the rage then) that had 'undone itself' and had it redone a week before the wedding with disastrous consequences. There were no blow driers in those days and her West End hairdresser had made a bad job even worse by re-perming her hair using smaller perming rollers and a stronger perm solution. She spent the entire morning trying to pull the tight, frizzled curls over her high forehead. There was still time but no make-up on yet and she was beginning to look like Harpo Marx. Thank god the wedding service was booked for 4pm.*

*Georgia was 24 now and rarely saw her father. She had been afraid to ask if he would give her away. He seemed so distant and she was so unsure of herself she didn't want to press him. She didn't want to press him? It was her wedding day and she needed to ask if he would be giving her away? He told her he would be round on the morning of the wedding to take some photos but after that? She simply didn't know.*

*Unannounced, Tom arrived that morning to take photos. He was a keen photographer with his own dark room and although it was late Autumn in Hainault, the sun was shining in the garden and the magnolia tree was in full bloom. He stayed about half an hour, taking most of the pictures in front of the tree and Georgia was too busy to notice if her parents had spoken to each other as he headed for the front door saying "See you later" as he left. She only hoped she would see him for the service.*

*As Tom left Georgia was side-tracked by her cousin asking her to show him around their new house and as she passed her mother in the hallway talking to Tom's brother, she heard her say, "I've always fancied you" as she continued to walk up the stairs with that sickening feeling again. Was her mother sex mad? Did she have no control over who she chose to flaunt herself at? Her mother was coming onto her ex-husband's brother, on her wedding day. It was more bizarre than ever but Georgia had to ignore it. She mustn't make a fuss, especially today. She knew Sylvie would only ridicule her or say 'you're lying,' in front of everyone.*

*Suddenly it was time to go. Larry had hired what he had been told was Mick & Bianca Jagger's wedding car. "It's a light blue and black vintage Rolls Royce. You'll love it" he'd said but as she glanced out of the window it looked like a hearse. She was horrified. Was this a sign of things to come?*

*To her surprise, her mother was already in the car. Somewhere back in time she had assumed Sylvie would be going with other members of the family and Tom would travel with her on this special day. She hadn't dared asked beforehand and now it was too late. They travelled the 30-minute journey in complete silence.*

*The wedding service was held in Finsbury Park, North London and as they drove up to the entrance Georgia saw people she didn't recognise milling around and thought she must be too early. There must be another wedding still going on and asked the driver to go "round the block, please." It turned out that the people were relatives she hadn't seen for so long that she simply didn't recognise them now. As she walked in, there were plenty of familiar faces, including her father. What a relief.*

*He looked perfect but he looked worried and he was sweating. She found out later that Larry and his family had still not arrived and, as his parents only lived a few minutes away, maybe he thought she was being jilted at the altar?*

*Before she knew it she was walking down the aisle with Tom. His hand felt so strong in hers. She was so proud of him being there. It felt so good to be by his side. This was the closest she had ever felt towards him and it was to be the nearest she ever got, never to hold his hand again.*

*After the service Larry explained why he was late. Weeks earlier, he had had the sleeves of his wedding jacket shortened and hadn't bothered to take the suit out of its protective bag until the morning of the wedding. It was only as he was putting his arm through the sleeve that he discovered that one of the sleeve linings had been sewn across the arm, making it impossible for him to put on.*

His mother had to unstitch, then re-stitch and press the sleeve, which is why they were all so late.

They had booked the Chanticleer Banqueting Suite, adjoining the Tottenham Hotspurs football ground at White Hart Lane and hired a great band for the reception. The music was good but the food was not. Sandwiches were not the usual wedding fayre, but it was all they could afford. Tom left soon after the meet and greet line up, saying something about his son having chickenpox. It must have been very difficult for him there Georgia thought, finally facing Sylvie's family.

As she went around the tables talking to everyone, an old friend of Larry's called to her, "Georgia, come here," with a stern look on his face. "What's the matter?" she asked. "It's my wife, she's very upset. She's spilt the soup down her new dress." Georgia looked puzzled. There was no soup, only sandwiches. Oh, great joke, what a shame she heard it first-hand though. She let it pass but there was always one regret on that day...she never danced with her father.

By now Tom had now moved in with Rita. They'd had a baby boy and Georgia knew he had built himself a new life with them. Rita had a daughter from her first marriage who was around Georgia's age and she assumed he had let the girl take her place and just didn't love her anymore. Her mother reassured her he was no loss. "He always wanted a boy, anyway" she said.

## CHAPTER NINE

# THE GOOD NEWS
# AND THE BAD NEWS

*Settling down to married life, Georgia had given up the job as bus conductor after a close shave with a penknife-wielding teenager who got on her bus while she was waiting for the driver to start their shift. She had noticed him standing at the bus stop and taking the knife out of his trouser pocket and put it up his sleeve as he boarded the bus. She knew then, it was time to leave the job and simply got off the bus, walked back to the bus garage, handed in her cash bag and told them she was resigning, right there. Not one of her better qualities she knew, giving up a well-paid job, but she saw no reason to continue working in a dangerous environment. Resignations were part of her career.*

*After temping as a legal sec in the City, Georgia found a job in a local solicitor's office. She liked the job. It was a small practice and the work was easy with no stress and not long after the wedding her mother moved to Peterborough, still some 90 miles away, selling the mobile home in some bizarre arrangement to Tom. Georgia never knew the exact arrangement they had about it. Sylvie was now living in a two-bedroomed flat in this new town in Cambridgeshire and Georgia assumed things between her and the Newcastle guy had fizzled out now and Sylvie had said she "wanted to be near family." She had a couple of cousins in Peterborough.*

*Larry and her mother were still not getting on although when they were in each other's company they did make the effort to be pleasant, with him never failing to make whispered observations to Georgia that there was something "fundamentally missing in her." They were fortunately rarely in the same room together.*

*1979 and Georgia was sitting at her desk at work when she started feeling nauseous. Her period was two weeks late and at lunchtime she went into the local chemist and bought a pregnancy test. She didn't know what feeling pregnant was like but something told her she was and the test confirmed she was correct. That Thursday evening she told Larry, who was delighted. He called his parents and Georgia called her mother. She seemed genuinely happy about it and invited them both for lunch on Sunday.*

*Georgia tried contacting Tom that evening too, and all that Friday and Saturday at the factory. In the years before mobile phones, it was the only number she had for him and guessed he must be at the mobile home in Braintree. Maybe she'd catch him at the factory on Sunday. He often worked weekends but she had no luck that Sunday. She kept ringing the factory right up to the time they left for lunch at her mother's. The weather was miserable, windy and raining driving all the way on the M11. They were glad to get out of the car as her mother greeted them with a friendly smile and said lunch was ready. They had just sat down to eat when the doorbell rang. Her mother said she wasn't expecting anyone as she went to the front door. She was back within seconds, shouting at the top of her voice "I knew this would happen. I was told this was going to happen." They both looked at her as if she had gone crazy when two police officers walked into the room behind her.*

*One of them smiled nervously, "I'm afraid I have some bad news" he said. Tom had been killed in a car crash just a few hours earlier. "You must be mistaken" Georgia responded, questioning the surname he had given her* father. "Why would you come to this address anyway? This is his ex-wife's place. It must be someone else." The older officer explained they had been called to the crash and had found a letter from Sylvie to him in his jacket pocket and it had her address on it, which led them to her. They left as quickly as they had appeared.

Suddenly, her mother started ranting again, "I was warned. I was warned years ago about this tragedy." Apparently she had been to a fortune teller in a seaside town over 20 years ago who told her this would happen.

Suddenly they were all feeling distraught. Larry thought it best if they were to go home and take Sylvie with them. At least they could all be together. But Sylvie wouldn't hear of it and insisted on staying put. The two of them left Peterborough late that night. It was the worst journey they can remember. It was raining hard on the unlit motorway all the way and it seemed to take forever before they felt safe, back home.

The next day it was Georgia who broke the news to her father's family. Her grandfather helped arrange the things that have to be arranged for funerals. Being pregnant, she was told, means she MUST stay at home on the day of the funeral. Something to do with 'a bad omen.' She felt so numb. She couldn't think straight. She didn't argue. She NEVER argued. She recalled later a vague memory of celebrations going on outside about a woman being voted the first female prime minister in the UK but she felt as if someone had ripped her arms from her body. A minister came, prayers were said, people tried to comfort her and then everyone was gone and she was left with the emptiness and finality only a child feels when a parent is gone. She hadn't even told him she loved him, although her heart said he knew. He was 51 and she never danced with him at her wedding, exactly 6 months earlier, to the day.

Weeks later there was an inquest and Georgia attended, alone, hoping it would help her come to terms with Tom's sudden departure. She heard a witness describe what had happened that day. His car had skidded at speed on the wet road, hitting a telegraph pole and killing him instantly. Exhibit 'A' was a completely bald tyre taken from the car. That didn't surprise her. She remembered the two wires together behind the dashboard and him saying he'd lost his keys. The policeman who attended the scene of the accident also spoke of the two passengers in the car at the time. Rita had sustained a serious injury to her hand and Scott, their 9-year-old son that Georgia had never met, had broken a leg. She couldn't make any sense of it. Why did HE have to die? It was so unfair. Two strangers had survived and her father was dead. She was still numb and shocked that a life could end so suddenly.

Sylvie had kept away. She made no contact whatsoever before, during and after the funeral. Even when Georgia rang her about the inquest she seemed uninterested and thought she must be devastated too. Georgia empathised. She knew her mother had always loved him but couldn't show her feelings to anyone now. These were Sylvie's feelings anyway and she never actually discussed these with her. Georgia knew his death was too sensitive a subject to discuss. It wouldn't have changed the facts anyway. Tom was never going to see his grandchild and *there was no chance of ever getting closer to him. He was gone for good.*

*Sarah was born eight months later. A perfect little girl with masses of dark hair and eyelashes so long, they were curled under when the nurse handed her to Georgia. And what a joy she would have been to Tom. Georgia's own grandfather dying just months before their second daughter, Sophie, was born. Another beautiful child they would have both been proud of and doted over. Perhaps they are somewhere near. She missed them both dearly.*

*Sophie's birth was easy and fast. Thirty minutes to be precise. Again, like Sarah, she had a full head of dark hair, perfectly formed and screaming like crazy. Her birth was the only time Georgia can recall her mother ever praising her. While she was in the hospital a beautiful flower arrangement arrived with a card saying "Who is a clever girl. Lots of love Mum xxx." She remembered it so very well. It was the only time she'd ever said something nice about her daughter and she often looked at the card to remind her she wasn't dreaming.*

*Sylvie loved seeing her granddaughters and constantly asked Georgia to bring them up to see her in Peterborough. Loading a baby and toddler in the car, making sure she had everything they could possibly need for the hour's journey on her own was one thing, but the thought of that motorway, the same one they had used after the news about her father, always in the rain it seemed, made Georgia decline more often than not. She didn't have the use of the car most days anyway. Larry had to take it to his parent's house in London each morning to pick up the taxi which he shared with his father.*

*Eventually, as the girls grew her mother's visits became more frequent. Larry and his brother started a new business together selling jewellery in Chapel Street Market in Islington on Saturdays and very occasionally her mother would come down and say Georgia could go with them. Her Saturday visits became more and more regular. "Don't get any ideas about me baby-sitting" she said. "I'll come down and look after the children when I want to and that's all."*

*It was great that the girls were in safe hands and what a relief to have the occasional break. No one else offered. Larry's parents said they 'lived too far away' and preferred to visit only for birthdays and Christmas. Babysitting was not offered and Georgia had only asked them if they could babysit once when Larry and her had the flu. "If you can't look after your own children, you shouldn't have them" was her mother-in-law's reaction. Georgia wanted to take the girls more often to see Sylvie but it was always so difficult with the one car and the girls at nursery and a whole ton of other stuff that goes on with toddlers. She wanted her mother to be closer anyway. Not for help, but just to be closer. She'd always kept her distance and she was constantly battling with herself. Could she do the journey or was it best to stay at home?*

*She had another battle with herself too. Mother's Day. Damned Mother's Day. How Sylvie used to go on about how all the other mothers she knew were given such beautiful bouquets of flowers from their daughters on*

*Mother's Day. But Georgia had stopped sending cards for Mother's Day over recent years. "What's wrong with you? I want at least a card!" she'd say and Georgia felt so very guilty. Why couldn't she bring herself to send her a card? Deep down she knew but couldn't say. How could she explain that she wanted to give her gifts and cards because she WANTED to, not because her mother INSISTED. Mother's Day was always a stalemate. Sylvie would go on and on about all the other mothers and Georgia would stay silent, lost for words, again.*

*Her birthdays were the same. She would tell Georgia in advance what she wanted and she would just go to the shop and buy it. One year she told her (never asking) that she wanted a new dressing gown. She gave Georgia her orders before she had the chance to ask what she wanted and felt obligated to follow her instructions. In the end she didn't even want to buy it but she knew she had no choice and no voice in the matter. Her opinion didn't count for anything but she didn't want to cross her. She was her mother.*

*She bought what she thought was a lovely dressing gown but when she gave it to her she looked at it disapprovingly, just like the handbag, flowers and other gifts Georgia had bought especially for her over the years, saying it wasn't what she wanted. Each time she tried to please her she felt like her mother was trying to take more and more advantage of her authority over her. Georgia was always left feeling guilty and worthless. She didn't know if she kept the dressing gown or any of her offerings but she always gave her the receipt in anticipation of an exchange or refund.*

*There were so many times when Larry would try and explain to her why she was feeling so bad about herself after being with her mother. He could see the unhappiness and depression she was going through but Georgia couldn't see it herself. They used to spend so many nights talking about the problem, trying to resolve it, but it always ended the same way. He would say something about Sylvie that she didn't agree with and they would argue into the early hours of the morning, going to bed angry and upset, all because Georgia was instinctively defending her mother.*

*Their animosity grew and the late nights arguing began to take a toll on Larry's work. It was getting more and more difficult for him to get up at 4am, working the late shift on the taxi and the stress began to show with Georgia staying locked in resentment for Larry against her mother for what amounted to many years. Whenever she had a problem, Larry would always refer to Sylvie and her lack of compassion. Georgia just never understood the point he was trying to make and put it all down to the classic problem that he simply didn't like his mother-in-law.*

*But now Larry was telling her what to do. While she had looked to him for support and protection their relationship soon changed from husband and wife to guardian and child. She became more and more nervous around him and built up an image of him as an ogre, determined to get his own way. Their relationship deteriorated daily.*

*In desperation, she confided in her mother for some guidance. "Divorce him" she said. "He's never been any good for you." She knew her hopes of 'learning to love him' were starting to dwindle. Georgia felt in her heart that the marriage was coming to an end. Her attempts at learning to love him had turned into learning to see the real Larry. His love for her was now controlling and she needed to be free. But what about the children? She had made a solemn promise to herself that she would never put them through the misery she had experienced with her own parents' divorce. She couldn't put them through it. She had made her bed and there was simply no other choice.*

*When Sylvie occasionally asked how she was getting on Georgia shared her thoughts and fears and how difficult it was for her to stand up for herself and say the things she really felt, just like when her and Tom were getting divorced. This was the first time she had broached this subject with Sylvie and began describing how unbearable the divorce had been for her at the time and for years after and that she knew there was nothing she could have done or said to change anything. "You should have said something at the time!" Sylvie interrupted her. "Maybe it would have made a difference. Maybe we would still be together now." Georgia felt sick, so guilty and worthless again.*

*That night in bed she told Larry what her mother had said. He was outraged. "How could she dump so much responsibility onto a 15-year-old? She's not fit to be a mother!." His hang-up with his mother-in-law was getting worse. He couldn't be right. She knew her mother had her best interests at heart, and now she was growing further and further away from Larry.*

*"Larry's just trying to turn you against me" her mother said after Georgia had divulged their last argument to her. Sylvie had never liked Larry and now she had the proof she wanted. Georgia had to agree.*

*Constantly reminding herself of the bed she had made, Georgia tried to keep everything to herself, but it was hard for a naturally open and honest person. It seemed as if every time she made an observation or stated a fact, it caused someone a problem, somewhere. She believed she had got everything completely wrong and was not fit to have opinions or discussions about her life with others. It would be better all round if she just kept quiet. Everyone would be better off, especially her girls.*

*One October afternoon, Georgia and her mother attend the funeral of a distant elderly relative. This was Georgia's first visit to the cemetery where her father was buried. She had been too upset to visit his grave until now. This funeral service was poignant and moved her to tears. She started to sob quietly as the 100 strong crowd stood in the prayer house. Immersed in her own sorrow, it was a relief to let out the pain she had held in for seven years. Suddenly, she was jolted back to the present tense as her mother dug her elbow into Georgia's rib cage, whispering with gritted teeth, "Don't be so stupid! Stop crying! What's the matter with you?" Stopping immediately she thought she must be showing a weakness of some kind that her mother did not approve of. Sylvie must be right. 'She's had more experience of such things than she could have had,' she thought. She was 32 years old and still obeying her mother, unquestioningly.*

Georgia sent her mother a birthday card wishing she didn't have to be reminded to do it. It would have felt better if Sylvie could trust her judgement, just like Georgia did with her own daughters. Sylvie did always send Georgia a birthday card without fail and on one occasion she had handed her the card smiling. "What's so funny?" Georgia asked. She said she was remembering buying the card. She had gone shopping with her sister Mary and they couldn't find a suitable card. "We had had such a laugh trying to find the right card for you when all we could find were cards 'to a loving daughter' and 'a caring daughter" she continued, "...it was ages before we found the right one." Georgia looked at the card, "To you daughter, on your birthday." Why was she treating Georgia like this? It was so cruel. What had she done to make her think so bad of her?

## CHAPTER TEN

# IT'S A WONDERFUL LIFE

*As years rolled on Sylvie's thoughts must have turned to the future. She said she'd like to live nearer to Georgia and her only grandchildren. Georgia couldn't believe it. Sylvie wanted to be near her after all these years. She was coming home and enlisted Georgia to find a suitable place to move to.*

*It took a few months and after scouring the local area and newspapers Georgia found a small ground floor flat opposite Hainault Forest with views of open fields and just a short walk to the neighbouring shops, with the busy high street a short bus ride away. Sylvie came down and looked around. "Yes, I'd like to live here" she said. Georgia knew her mother would be happy here, just a couple of miles away from her and happily proceeded to scrub the place from top to bottom, ready for her mother on moving day.*

*After moving day, Georgia brought her back home for dinner and opened the bottle of champagne Mum's friend Neil had given her for her 21ˢᵗ birthday that she had been keeping for a really special occasion. This was the best reason ever. Her mother had come home and they could begin to be one happy family, on Sylvie's terms, of course. The children were thrilled too. They would be seeing her much more regularly and were already making plans to visit her. This was wonderful.*

*Sylvie bought herself a puppy that summer after her cat had died. Everyone fell in love with friendly, inquisitive, bold and energetic Tramp, but after just a few months Georgia noticed on each visit how the dog had become nervous and timid, cowering in its basket. She passed it off as some bad experience it must have had in the past and ignored it.*

*But Georgia was horrified as she watched and heard how Sylvie treated it. The same way she was treated as a child. The tone of her voice and the words she used. It was like going back in time. Sylvie was chastising the dog just as she had done Georgia, and for no good reason. Within a few months, Georgia noticed a change come over her too and preferred not to be in her mother's company for too long. She was becoming more depressed than ever.*

*It was a few months later when Georgia noticed a change coming over the girls after visiting Sylvie. They had complained that nanny never believed them if they said they had a tummy ache or something hurt. They said she told them they were "being silly" and Georgia knew exactly what they meant, explaining "She's always dismissed anything I've said too. Don't worry about it, it's just her way. Nanny grew up in a time when children were not allowed an opinion. She just can't help it" trying to reassure them, adding "phone me if you're worried about anything when you're there."*

*Sarah was 11 when she called Georgia from Sylvie's place one afternoon just as Georgia got back home. It was strange hearing her daughter's young voice on the phone, "Can you pick us up?" she whispered. "Are you alright? What's the matter?" she asked, "I just don't feel very well" Sarah replied.*

*She drove back, greeted by her mother with folded arms who was already standing by the open front door, "There's nothing wrong with her" she said. "I can tell. Her eyes are not glazed and she was running around half an hour ago." But the girls were now standing outside the front door with their coats on. Georgia said "I'll speak to you later, mum" and walked the girls to the car. On the way home Sarah said "I'd rather not see nanny anymore" and they both started to cry. Georgia was puzzled and said "Let's talk about this when we get home." She was sure there was nothing for them to be upset over. It must just be a misunderstanding.*

*Sitting at the kitchen table, Sarah told her that not only did nanny not believe them when they had a pain but that she was saying bad things about Georgia too. Sophie now 8, nodded as she continued. Unbeknown to Georgia, the girls had often questioned Sylvie about why she thought their mother was so 'bad,' but she always dismissed their questions. Georgia wanted to know more. "What kind of things was she saying about me?" quizzing them both. "Oh, just that you're a bad daughter and you're not a very nice person," Sarah blubbered. Shocked at what the girls had said, Georgia went upstairs to her bedroom, closed the door and rang her mother, confronting her with what she had just heard. "You're mad! You're imagining things! I wouldn't say anything to hurt those children. I haven't said anything bad about you" Sylvie yelled. But Georgia knew the girls wouldn't make this up. Something had to be done.*

*That evening after dinner, Larry, Georgia and the girls discussed at length the situation at nanny's. The girls couldn't (or wouldn't) say exactly what Sylvie was saying about Georgia or why she was bad but it was upsetting them. 'Maybe that's why they were having tummy aches so often at her place?' Georgia thought.*

*She had questioned her mother each time the children came home upset and she always denied any knowledge of it, saying she hadn't said a word against her. Larry and her decided the girls should have a break from seeing her until she could find out exactly what was going on. The following day she paid her mother a visit alone, intending to extract whatever information she could about what she had been saying to the children. Sylvie sat in her usual chair, arms folded as Georgia stood in front of her, asking what the hell she was saying. Now Sylvie had that look again, the one with the stary eyes, getting angrier and with no hesitation put her fingers in her ears and sang, yes sang "La, la, la, la, can't hear you" at the top of her voice. Georgia felt her head swell and with the frustration of being lost for words, picked up a cushion from the sofa and looked right into Sylvie's now terror-filled eyes. Perhaps a few seconds more and she would have smothered her with it, but coming to her senses quickly, Georgia threw the cushion across the floor and slammed the front door behind her as she left.*

*Georgia rang her some days later to tell her that the girls would not be visiting so often because of the things she was saying to them about her. There and then, Georgia witnessed for herself what her mother had been saying. "You ARE a bad person. You are stopping my grandchildren from seeing me." She was beginning to see the real opinion Sylvie had of her. The girls didn't want to see her at all but at least she had been trying to resolve the problem. It couldn't continue as it was but her mother was in complete denial of her part in it.*

*Georgia thought her mother would start to understand eventually and tried to get the girls to visit her but they were adamant. What could she or Larry do? Somewhere in the back of her mind she felt it was all her fault. It had to be her to blame. She was bad. Her mother had said so to her and to her grandchildren. Georgia had confirmation from all angles. Her marriage was on the rocks, her children were living without one of their grandparents and she had ostracized herself from her very own mother. She wasn't worth anything.*

*Georgia stopped speaking. Quite suddenly she just stopped. She couldn't bear the sound of her own voice anymore. It felt like she was shouting when she tried to speak and it was a relief staying silent. She stayed silent for weeks and also stayed in the same armchair just staring in space most days, with no thoughts, just trying to bring as little attention to herself as possible. She did what was necessary for Larry and the girls but the rest of the time she went back to staring into space in her armchair in the corner of the lounge.*

*It was soon after that she stopped washing. Her hair, body, clothes, everything. She was worthless. She had even cut her hair as short as possible so that it needed no attention. Her life was grinding to a halt. There was no point in doing anything. Everyone else around her was what mattered. Even strangers in the street. They all looked like really important people, heads of huge corporations, VIP's. She wasn't worth wasting water on and saved it for everyone else to use.*

*She ate the bare minimum of food. No excesses. Photos taken at the time showed her in a state of anorexia. Georgia was a pathetic excuse for a human being and she knew it. She hoped one day soon someone would just turn a switch and she'd be gone, away from this living hell.*

*Georgia hit rock bottom at 38 and Larry knew he had to step in after seeing her physically and mentally deteriorate so much. Her state of mind couldn't be ignored anymore. He'd been trying to help her with his guidance, hoping she'd snap out of it but she had chosen to ignore it.*

*The GP told her 'You're suffering from depression.' I'm sending you to see someone. The psychiatrist prescribed anti-depressants and said she'd feel better in a few weeks. Ok. It was official she had depression and it was treatable.*

*Georgia had very little dealings with her mother during that time and six weeks of Prozac produced a new feeling in her. She felt her heart lift a little. She became daring. Instead of walking the dog in the park, she gave him an extra fast run by attaching his lead to her bicycle and pedalled like crazy. She began waking up a little earlier each morning instead of sleeping all day. Very slowly she started to come back to life again and even heard herself laugh out loud, shocked at the realisation that she hadn't laughed in years.*

*She was feeling stronger and sitting on the park bench one morning, arms outstretched behind her, she felt the* wind run through her fingers. The wind had touched her. She felt honoured. She had never felt so happy before and even though the experience was fleeting it was profound and she wanted more. She wanted to keep that happiness and by now the psychiatrist was pleased with her progress and discharged her from his clinic. She knew she still had a long way to go to resolve the issues with her marriage and her mother. "I'm going to refer you to a psychologist who specialises in this type of thing. I'm sure she can help." he said reassuringly.

The clinical psychologist would be a good way forward.

## CHAPTER ELEVEN

# TREADING NEW GROUND

*Georgia went alone to see Janice for the first time in the Psychology Department, although some of the following appointments were with Larry. The sessions continued for 9 months, "the time it takes to make a new person" one of Larry's aunts had noted.*

*Bringing her up to date in no time, Georgia felt comfortable with Janice and hoped she could give her answers to some of her problems. Janice had found the observation she had made about her mother's puppy very interesting and thought it was extremely significant. "It's a classic case" she said. "You've allowed your mother to dictate her will to you." She could see what she meant but how could she go against her own mother? Surely, she would be rejected by society once they knew she opposed her own mother. Taking Janice through her life's history while she listened, making no judgements, Georgia was able to confront herself with the facts. In just a few months she knew there were too many instances where her mother was wrong and not right. There was no denying the things she had said or done and yes, they were real events but "Surely," she asked Janice, "my mother had good reason to treat me like that. She was only acting the way a mother could when dealing with a bad daughter."*

*"Why are you bad?" Janice asked. "I don't know" Georgia replied. "I must have done something really awful a long time ago because, for the life of me, I can't remember what it was that I did." She knew exactly what Janice was going to say next and held her breath "Perhaps you should ask her. Ask her what you said that was so bad."*

*Georgia knew in the back of her mind that day would come and by coincidence only a few days after seeing Janice, she had a call from one of her mother's oldest friends. John and his wife Jackie stayed in touch with Sylvie and knew things were bad between them both and suggested they may be able to help by being the "referees" if they could all meet. Georgia almost cried. "I'd welcome you with open arms" she replied. At last, someone wanted to get them together. Her mother had only rejected her again a few days earlier but Georgia really believed things were going to start looking up. She knew it was time to ask that question soon.*

*John and Jackie agreed to bring Sylvie over to Georgia's house Thursday evening and she was looking forward to finally sorting this all out, once and for all. The girls said hello to everyone and then went up to their rooms while Larry showed them into the lounge. Georgia was waiting for them and Larry made some polite conversation while she made the tea and as soon as Georgia came in, she was ready to speak.*

*It was February 1992, and Georgia was 38 years old and had been dreading asking this question for fear of the response but, standing in front of the unlit fireplace, out it came "Is it right that you think I am a bad daughter?" directing the question to her mother. "Yes" Sylvie replied. "Well, I need to know why. What did I do that makes you feel the way you do towards me? It must have been something pretty bad but I can't remember what I did." She felt her whole body go cold and numb as she was about to be told what she had done so long ago that must have been so dreadful and held her breath. "Oh, you did more than one thing" Sylvie replied. "When you were 14 you told me I had B.O. I have never forgotten that and will never forgive you. How dare you? And when I came out of hospital after my hysterectomy you didn't help me with the housework. You didn't even come to see me in the hospital. You're sick. There must be something seriously wrong with you!" Georgia noticed Jackie's open mouth drop almost to the floor. John was motionless. Georgia was shocked and suddenly, everything made sense. For the first time in her life, Georgia's mother was wrong and SHE was right. Her mother was correct in that Georgia's informed of her of her B.O., as a 14 years old girl would say in innocence to her mother. And she did go and visit Sylvie at the hospital, but she was asleep and Georgia didn't want to disturb her. This evening had suddenly given Georgia an enormous insight into her mother's state of mind. She had taken Georgia's comments as personal criticism and this was a major breakthrough as Georgia began to see the real Sylvie.*

*After the meeting the girls were still reluctant to visit Sylvie and Georgia let it rest for a while and within two weeks Sylvie called one Saturday morning for a chat (yes, a chat) just as Georgia was putting clean sheets on the bed. Stopping what she was doing she sat down as Sylvie chatted away, telling her how she and her family had all been out celebrating the arrival of Georgia's first cousin and her new husband, over from the States. They had all gone out for dinner the night before, apparently arranged by Sylvie's sister-in-law, Lou. There were three first cousins but only 2 had been out for dinner that night. The other one was Georgia and she hadn't been invited.*

As the news hit her, she started to sob. Her mother didn't seem to understand the importance of what she had just said. "What on earth's the matter with you?" she asked. Georgia put the phone down and picking it up again dialled Lou's number. "Why wasn't I invited to the family dinner last night?" she cried. "I'm really sorry," Lou said, "I thought your mother was going to ask you. I just assumed she asked you and you couldn't come." By now Georgia was sobbing so hard she couldn't hold the phone any longer and dropped it to the floor. She couldn't speak and her head was hurting so much it felt like it was going to burst.

The girls were now in her bedroom, trying to comfort her but she had to wave them away. The feeling of rejection and frustration was destroying her and she didn't want them to see her like this or be any part of this misery. Larry was out working that morning and she badly needed his support. She felt so alone. She couldn't stop sobbing and it reminded her of her father on the stairs, sobbing all those years ago.

She'd lost all sense of time sitting on the edge of the bed and only stopped crying when she felt someone sit down beside her. It was her mother who was just about to put her arm around her when Georgia shrieked her away. It was unbearable as she flinched, saying "Leave me alone!" Sylvie looked puzzled and said "I really can't see what was wrong with you not being with the family last night. I never even thought to ask you," she began, "I think you're being very silly about this anyway." Sylvie had no idea what she had done. She genuinely believed there was no wrong on her part and the frustration of Georgia not being *listened to now was becoming intolerable. Georgia was now more hostile towards her than ever.*

*As time went on Georgia noticed she could cope with life as long as Sylvie wasn't around, but that wasn't the answer. Now it was time for action. She **had** to make her listen and assert herself, stand up to her and sort this out once and for all. She drove to her flat, ready to insist that she listen to what she had to say. It could only make things better. Better for both of them together, and the girls. A relationship with no bad feelings. She knew Sylvie must want the same and all she had to do was explain her point of view clearer, then she could start to build a **real** relationship, just like the mothers and daughters Sylvie had spoken of so often. All Georgia wanted Sylvie to do was listen.*

*Sylvie let her in and then sat in her chair with the folded arms again, glaring as Georgia felt the adrenalin pumping in the right side of her neck, her breathing becoming deeper and stronger. Remaining standing in front of her, she started to explain this pattern of conflict they kept repeating. She spoke quietly and gently "I want us to have a real relationship. Just listen to me, please." Still sitting, Sylvie turned the whole top half of her body away, again covering her ears with her hands as she moved. "I've got the perfect life. I don't want to know," her mother screamed.*

*The frustration of seeing her mother physically close herself off to her was so frustrating and was too much to bear anymore. Georgia walked out into the rain and got in the car. Nothing made sense. How could she say she had the perfect life? Georgia was going through agony because her mother didn't want to share her life with her. Why did she turn away? Why couldn't she listen? It was such an impossible situation. How could she get through to someone who didn't want her to? Georgia stopped washing again and had never felt this worthless before.*

*She decided to go and visit her mother's old friends John and Jackie again. She had seen them a few times after what she called "the B.O. evening" and told them how worthless she was feeling and how she was neglecting herself whenever she had contact with her mother. Could they explain to her mother the importance of talking? Maybe they could suggest her meeting an independent counsellor? Sylvie needed help, professional help this time. They said they'd speak to her and Georgia left full of hope. It was the last time she spoke to them.*

*The scene at her mother's kept repeating itself in her mind. Why did she turn her back on her? Why wouldn't she listen? How could she say she had the perfect life? How could it be perfect without her in it, or at least the girls, her only grandchildren? She **must** want them in her life. But deep down, Georgia felt she, herself must be making something out of nothing. After all, if her mother didn't care about her then why should she?*

## CHAPTER TWELVE

# ON THE UP ...
# OR DOWN?

It was the end of the summer holidays and the girls had just gone back to school when an official looking letter arrived in the post. It was a summons from the local Magistrate's Court for Georgia to appear before them. Her mother was taking her to court requesting a contact order to see the children. Sylvie had accused her of stopping them from seeing her. It had only been a few weeks since she had seen John and Jackie to suggest Sylvie and Georgia both see a professional counsellor. She will never know if they misunderstood what she meant or whether her mother missed the point altogether. Whatever the reason, she knew she could never confide in her mother's friends again.

Sylvie had instructed a local solicitor and Georgia was so flabbergasted at the summons that she immediately sat at the kitchen table and wrote a seven-page letter in response, explaining the problems the two of them had had for so many years and that she wasn't trying to stop the children from seeing their grandmother and that it was actually her mother that was perpetuating the situation. All they needed to do was talk together and everything would be sorted. Adding that it **was** the girl's' choice not to see their grandmother and that if she couldn't agree to sorting it all out between them, the girls would have to attend the court as it was their choice not to see her, not Georgia's.

The solicitor's response was heartless with more unfounded accusations about her character. Georgia called his office to see if he'd actually read her letter. The response was cruel. He said he thought she was some kind of wicked mother. Her mother had convinced him Georgia was evil. Did Sylvie and her solicitor realise they *were both sabotaging every attempt Georgia made to save the relationship? Again she suggested some kind of mediation but he wasn't interested. He said he didn't believe a single word she said. Not only was she being ignored again but it seemed every ounce of hope was being crushed out of her. She felt like the enemy and her head was hurting again.*

*She tried to reason with her mother several times more, but she wouldn't budge. She called her to explain about the girls having to attend the court for this hearing but it had no effect whatsoever.*

*Larry's brother and wife, Paul and Debbie had recently moved just down the road and Georgia had confided in Debbie after she had shown concern for Georgia's health and fortunately, when it was explained that the hearing was taking place tomorrow, Debbie and Larry went to Sylvie's, asking her to withdraw her instructions before it was too late. And they must have got through to her. She must have listened to them because suddenly, the case was dropped.*

*Georgia had tried to keep things from the girls. She'd always told them the truth about whatever they wanted to know, unlike her mother when she was younger. If only Sylvie knew she had no reason to worry about her daughter's influence over the girls. She didn't have influence over herself. She had no opinions of her own and could hardly make **any** decisions anymore.*

*But after all this, Georgia still thought highly of her mother. She knew she loved the children and their visits must have* been important. *She also knew she had been rejected now. That was official but even so, she still encouraged the girls to see her. After four years on, they still showed no sign of wanting anything to do with their grandmother and still feeling very guilty for the current situation it was only in the years to come that Georgia would see just how dangerously close she came to losing everything that mattered. Being condemned for something she never did brought much more stress and strain than she could have known. The frustration Georgia had endured was about to show itself.*

*Life was a little easier now Georgia had no need to see Janice, the psychologist anymore. She was coping with her family and she thought as long as she could do that, everything would be all right. She hadn't spoken to her mother since just before the court hearing over a year ago and at last she was beginning to feel better emotionally and was definitely on the way up and even started putting on a little weight, having recently giving up smoking.*

*1994 - Georgia was 40 years old, at home serving dinner one evening when she felt what can only be described as a sledge-hammer hit her on the right side of her head. She cried out in pain, ran into the lounge and, as if by instinct, threw the cushions to the floor and laid down flat on the sofa. She had never felt pain like this before. And this was serious. Larry was holding her hand as she started to cry "I think I'm going to die, right now!" she said as he stared back at her. Not even stopping to call an ambulance, he carried her into the car and drove to the nearest hospital at lightning speed. The A & E Department checked Georgia out for 7 hours, saying they couldn't find anything wrong* with her and that she was "actually in A1 shape" and gave her some pro-codomol tablets to cure a migraine. It took 4 days before a private neurologist was able to diagnose what had really happened and called for an ambulance to take her on a blue light to the London Hospital, as this private hospital had no facilities for "brain surgery".

Sliding into a CAT scanner, Georgia was promptly told she'd had a brain haemorrhage and shouldn't move a muscle because a second bleed was quite likely and could be fatal. She was put in the Royal (trauma) Ward and was instructed to lay completely still for two weeks, flat on her back while any 'spasms' subsided. No surgery could be undertaken until then. It's amazing how quickly you can learn to eat, drink and deal with every bodily function lying down without moving when the stakes are so high.

After being constantly told to 'Drink more water' through a straw, the neurosurgeon explained 'We have to treat the haemorrhage, it can't be ignored. It's a time bomb waiting to go off. You have a choice, either undergo major brain surgery here when the bleeding is under control or we can send you home and arrange for you to have laser treatment once a month in Leeds for two years. There is the 50-50 risk of paralysis, stroke, loss of speech or simply ending up a cabbage. There are, of course, the same risks and no guarantees with either option."' Gosh.

He left Larry and Georgia to mull over the choices but they both knew there was only one. Without hesitation Georgia agreed immediately that surgery now would be best. She couldn't bear the thought of walking around like a time bomb for two years. At least this would be over *soon. There was some mention of holes being drilled, head flaps, titanium clips and her head being shaved but Georgia reckoned it was all a small price to pay if she was to survive intact. She had already enjoyed a great sense of euphoria at simply surviving this near-death experience and was feeling surprisingly very positive about it all, even though her mother was constantly in the back of her mind. Just days before the op she broke down in front of a nurse, asking her advice. How could she make her mother listen? Was it possible for the hospital to arrange some kind of counselling for them both? The poor woman didn't know what to say. She was a highly trained nurse but not in the kind of treatment Georgia wanted.*

*The medical team were fantastic and she actually felt a fraud lying there, feeling better every day when around her were far more serious injuries. The middle-aged woman in the next bed had just arrived in London from Canada and had looked the wrong way as she crossed the road and had been knocked down by a double-decker bus. Georgia felt very lucky.*

*Then she had an idea. She phoned Larry. He was home that day making arrangements for the girls to stay with their friends so he could stay with Georgia after the operation. The hospital had agreed to a side bed next to hers for a couple of days. She asked him for Janice's number. Maybe she could see her and Sylvie together and looked around for the telephone trolley on wheels, asking the nurse to call the number for her. She was finally put through to Janice and telling her what had happened and that she was in hospital, Janice was shocked, insisting "One thing at a time. I wish you well and I am looking forward to hearing from you when you are fully recovered. Then I will be happy to see you both." Great!*

*She hadn't seen her mother for over two years when, just three days before the op, just as a nurse was doing her 'obs' Sylvie walked towards her. "Oh my god!" the nurse said, "your blood pressure has just hit the roof!" She knew why as she lay there motionless, feeling surprisingly awkward and uncomfortable. Her mother opened the conversation with "How are you?" Still feeling euphoric, Georgia replied "I feel fantastic!" smiling and feeling lucky to be alive. 'Being funny, are you?' Sylvie barked back. What? She was being sincere but Sylvie didn't believe her. Sylvie turned and left. Just like that.*

*Maybe it **did** sound like an odd thing to say but 'she came to see me. She cared and That's what's important' Georgia thought, feeling even better and more confident than ever that things would still work out, somehow.*

*Georgia told Larry to go home as they wheeled her to theatre. There was no point in hanging around but he was holding her hand tight and it took a stern-faced nurse to tell him 'I'm sorry, you're not allowed any further now, sir", as he let go and told her he loved her. As she lay on that trolley, she had a feeling of utter bliss come over her. It was like a huge blanket of cotton wool enveloping her. She had never felt so safe and peaceful in her entire life. What will be will be, she thought.*

*The anaesthetist asked her to count from one hundred backwards and she only got as far as 99 before coming round again in the recovery room after the five-hour operation. The nurse was waking her gently and lifting her arm, asked Georgia to squeeze her hand. She had woken with her wits about her. How was her left side? Was it ok? Did everything work like before? They smiled together as she squeezed her hand, "There's nothing wrong with you!" she grinned. 'Thank god' Georgia thought. She was strong again and could feel the difference. Every 15 minutes when the ob's were being performed, she grew stronger. "What is today? What's the capital of England? Where are you? Who's the prime minister?." How they laughed when she couldn't remember John Major's name but called him "The Grey Man." Sorry Mr. Major but that WAS your nickname!*

*There were so many get well cards. The bedside cabinet was overflowing with them and one morning she woke to find them all the way around the curtain rail of the bed. It felt like Christmas. Larry, the girls and friends were visiting every day. Gifts of flowers, bright red lipstick, head scarves, smoked salmon and cream cheese bagels, a blue and white knitted nurse her lovely Aunt Rosie had made and had travelled all the way from Canvey Island by public transport to see her. She didn't deserve this much attention but it was wonderful.*

*She was doing fine and wasn't at all surprised when she saw her reflection in the bathroom mirror. It wasn't too bad. The surgeon had only shaved three-quarters of her scalp, which she thought was a little odd, but the tiniest of scars that went from the top of her forehead, over her skull, to the top of her right ear would be hardly noticeable once her hair grew back. The swollen eyes and face were also temporary and her priorities in life now were reassuringly similar to those she had before the operation. Superficial imperfections were such a small price to pay for still being intact after a craniotomy.*

*She had to admit this was not one of her best looks and something told her she could use this 'face' as the greatest opportunity she was ever likely to have to make her mother listen to her. If she saw her like this she must let her speak. She **must** let her explain how they could start to work things out. She had to see Sylvie. Larry knew how stressful such a meeting could be and said she was in no fit state for such an encounter. But she felt strong and sure of herself. There was nothing to lose. It could only help. Georgia asked him to call her and tell her she needed to see her there at the hospital.*

## CHAPTER THIRTEEN

# DECISIONS, DECISIONS

Sylvie arrived at Georgia's bedside two days later, alone and looking quite amicable. It was a glorious, sunny day in July and now that Georgia was allowed out of bed, she walked her mother out onto the open balcony at the end of the ward. The chair she had taken out there the night before was still in the same place. There was a large statue of Queen Alexandra of the Netherlands in the garden below and Georgia loved to sit on the balcony in the early evening as the starlings began their nightly ritual of circling and swooping between the monument and the trees. She asked Sylvie, walking like a queen, to sit in the chair and went back into the ward, picked up and carried another chair onto the balcony. It was such a beautiful day. She knew it was a good sign and smiled nervously as she explained how unhappy she was and how Sylvie had to be prepared to face the past and go over it in detail. Without confronting all of this, they wouldn't be able to move on and she would be locked in resentment for her mother forever.

Sylvie let her speak, remaining silent, only giving an occasional nod in acknowledgement. At last, within a few minutes Georgia felt she had already got her back on her side. She was having a deep and meaningful conversation with her mother about their lives and for the first time she could ever remember, Sylvie didn't ignore her. Georgia spoke of her hopes for them both, for the future, the girls and her own personal dreams with Calligraphy. She opened herself totally and again, trusted that her mother would understand.

Two and a half hours later Georgia finished speaking. Neither of them could believe so much time had passed on the balcony. *Georgia said she couldn't remember the last time she had been able to spend two minutes in her mother's company and they laughed. What a relief. At last her mother was coming back to her way of thinking. It was worth her persevering.*

*Georgia had managed to explain to Sylvie the importance of getting someone to mediate between them and how much they had to gain from it if only she would give it a go. Sylvie confessed she was scared to drag up the past and wanted no part of it, refusing point blank to see anyone. Georgia told her it didn't matter how long it was going to take, she would wait until she was ready. All she had to do was call and they could even see Janice if she felt comfortable about it. They kissed each other goodbye and Georgia knew things would start to improve now. She loved her mother so much and she knew she had touched her heart that day.*

*November, four months later, Sylvie called her daughter. She was ready to see Janice. Georgia was so thrilled at the thought of finally sifting through the years of misunderstandings and condemnation and called Janice's office straight away.*

*Two weeks was a long time to wait but they were both now there, in the Psychology Department of the hospital and Georgia felt so exhilarated, her mother and her sitting in THIS waiting room. She was on cloud nine and couldn't believe it after all this time.*

*"I'd like to speak to Janice on my own" her mother whispered in her ear. "Fine, no problem" Georgia replied*

*without hesitation. "Whatever you want to do is ok. I'll introduce you and wait outside until you call me in."*

*Janice appeared from behind the waiting room door and gestured them to follow her. Georgia introduced her mother, saying she wanted to see her alone first and asked her to let her know when they were ready for her to join them. Standing by the window of the waiting room, Georgia watched a bird fly to a large tree planted in the hospital grounds. Autumn colours still remained but most of the leaves were on the ground as she heard the crunch of footsteps on a path somewhere. She was still elated. What did she care that her mother wanted to see Janice on her own first. It was all good and full of promise. Janice walked back into the waiting room five minutes later. "Come in, Georgia" she said.*

*Sitting in her usual chair now flanked by them both, Georgia was so looking forward to what was coming. Or so she thought. Janice waited for her to get comfortable and then proceeded, "Your mother has just told me she has the perfect life. She is very happy with her life and doesn't want anything to do with you or your children. She says she wants to stop this turmoil that you are putting her through." What? Georgia could hardly believe the words she was saying and turned to her mother "Are you saying you would rather live without me and the girls because your life is already so perfect?." The word "yes" came from her mouth but still not believing what she was hearing Georgia began to shout, "But don't you understand that the girls don't want to see you because you think so badly of me? Isn't it worth finding out what the problem is so that the girls will want to see you again? I want you to be close to them but you keep pushing them away!"*

*"It's too embarrassing to see them now" she said curtly. "What are you talking about? They're your grandchildren. What on earth are you embarrassed about?"*

*Janice had remained silent during this verbal exchange but even she was showing her frustration, "Georgia only wants what's natural for you all. She has expected you to want to get involved and help resolve this problem." Sylvie replied, "Yes, she expected that from me years ago when her and Larry had a big argument just before they got married. Georgia asked me to speak to Larry's mother to try and sort things out then. It's got nothing to do with me and I don't want any part of this rubbish!"*

*Janice tried again, "But Georgia was only asking you to do something that she thought her mother would be able to do. There is nothing wrong in her asking for your help." "I don't want to know about it anymore" she said and suddenly Georgia realised something she had never thought of before. They had always been alone together whenever Sylvie talked to her this way. That was until today. Today she had a witness and Janice may have even made notes about this meeting. Janice siding with Georgia's point of view was enough for her to know that her mother's attitude was wrong. Georgia wasn't mad. She wasn't stupid. Her feelings were correct and they always had been.*

*That day, all questions to Sylvie were futile. Her mother had switched off. There was nothing left but rejection.*

*Again. But they were so close to getting somewhere. What was she doing this for? Why couldn't she see how important this meeting was. Georgia felt the stab in her heart again, the one she had felt so many times before. It hurt so much and she didn't understand anything again. This can't be the end. There must be more. She must want more than this. But there was no more to say so Georgia got up, turning to Janice, "I'll be in touch" as she walked out of the room.*

*As she walked down the stairs into the long corridor to the car park she heard her mother's footsteps behind. She was glad to get into the frosty fresh air and as she headed to the car she saw a squirrel run across the grass and stopped to watch as it scooted along, then dart up a tree, thinking how great it must feel to be free of emotional stress. Her mother had caught up by now and spoke "I'm sorry I can't get involved but I still love you." It was at that precise moment she realised she felt nothing for her mother anymore. Her love had gone and there was nothing left. All her feelings for her mother had simply vanished. She couldn't even be bothered to speak to her.*

*She took Sylvie home in silence, which was pretty decent of her under the circumstances. There was a bus stop outside the hospital and she only lived a couple of miles away and Georgia could have easily left her to find her own way home but as always, she was so nice, so considerate.*

*As Georgia's car approached the flat Sylvie turned to her, "Keep in touch by phone so I can see how you're keeping." "No!" Georgia screamed, "No more! I will not let you bad mouth me and then act like some kind of concerned mother. Don't ever phone me again unless you are prepared to face the truth," scribbling Janice's phone number on a scrap of paper, pushing it into her hand. "Here's Janice's number. Take it. Sort yourself out and fuck off!" It was the first time she had ever sworn at her mother and it felt surprisingly good.*

*Sylvie looked at her in that puzzled way as she got out of the car and walked away, not looking back. Did she know the importance of what had just happened? As she drove home Georgia began to cry. Why? It was nothing new, what had just happened. Today was just like any other day in her mother's company.*

*"Well? How did it go?" Larry asked, greeting her with a big smile and eagerly awaiting her reply. "It didn't," she said. "It was a complete disaster" flopping into the armchair. "That's the last tear I'll ever shed for her. It's over. I've lost her."*

*Rightly or wrongly, she had tried to explain to the girls what had been going on between her and their grandmother previously, but how could she tell them what had happened today? The girls knew where she had been that day and came breezing in from school wanting to know immediately what had happened. She couldn't tell them the truth and said her "… and nanny had another argument but in time it will all be ok." She just couldn't tell them the truth. She knew it would have crushed them and instead said "I'm afraid we had another argument but in time it will all be ok." She just could not tell them any more than that and made herself a promise that day to never exclude her children from her life and her from theirs. There was a* sadness amongst the four of them as the outcome had left little to discuss and Georgia had no reason to remind the girls to visit nanny again. A few months later, Georgia received a letter from her mother:

Dear Georgia,

I have given a lot of thought to your wish for me to see your therapist again. It's my dearest wish that we can be on speaking terms with each other and able to phone each other from time to time. I'm your mum and I love you I always have, however I feel I'm not able to enter into sessions with your therapist. This is not to do with you. It's to do with me. I really hope you can understand. This is not a decision written in haste. This is how I feel at the moment. I just can't handle any emotional turmoil at the present time. Keep well, Love Mum

Georgia read it through a few times but she couldn't make much sense of it. Her love had drifted away the day she'd seen the squirrel. She **did** expect to be hit by a bolt of lightning or at least be punished with some paralysing illness for the rest of her life. How could she possibly be allowed a clear conscience after having no feeling left for her mother?

Was the unthinkable possible? Live a happy life ever after without her? But she was still reliving each rejection Sylvie had hurled at her. Was Georgia to spend the rest of her life haunted by these thoughts, still full of guilt and doubt? Did she remember everything in Janice's office clearly? But these were her mother's words, not hers. And she *had a witness who knew she never wanted anything other than a resolution between them.*

*The neurosurgeon at the hospital had explained how the burst blood vessel had caused the brain haemorrhage, but she knew there was more to it than that. The years of rejection, disappointment and frustration had taken their toll. It was emotional stress that had burst the vein, and despite that knowledge and even though her feelings for her mother had gone, she was still left with the same old guilt. Did Sylvie really say those things in Janice's office? Maybe her mind was making it worse than it really was. Still unsure of her responsibilities and herself. But they **were** her mother's words, not hers. And Georgia **did** have a witness.*

*So now she had a decision to make. Keep trying to get through to Sylvie, risking another haemorrhage or get on with her life without her in it? She just couldn't bear the thought and the answer was precisely that. The thought. It was thoughts in her mind that were paralysing her. She knew how genuine she had been in her endeavours and suddenly realised she had no need to hold on to these thoughts anymore. Her thoughts were her choice, no one else's. If her life was based on what she thought was right then she could live with herself and sleep at night without a guilty conscience. She had done everything she possibly could to resolve their differences but the outcome was because of her mother, not her. Sylvie had rejected everything Georgia had ever tried to do. Enough was enough now. Years of submission were slowly becoming apparent. Georgia's conditioned mind was starting to*

*think for itself.  Her mother was wrong and she was right.
What a revelation.*

*At first she felt she was betraying Sylvie but as the days
passed and as life got busy again, Georgia began to feel
comfortable without her mother in her life.  It was odd but
it felt right.  For the first time, at 40 years old, she felt she
was right and responded to the letter some weeks later.
"This will be" she thought, "the last contact I will ever have
with her" as she wrote:*

*Mum,*

*I received your letter.   It's a tragedy that you regard
understanding how our relationship got into such a mess
as emotional turmoil.  If only you knew the hurt and upset I
feel when you speak the way you do of me.  I know you're
not aware of it, but that doesn't mean you're not saying
these things.  And no, I'm not imagining these things.  I
used to believe it was my imagining how badly you thought
of me but, to be honest, whenever you speak to or of me,
you always manage to condemn me for something.*

*We are both to blame for the state of our relationship.  The
only difference is that at one time, I was a child and looked
to you for support.  You may think you gave it to me but
my interpretation of it was not the same.*

*There are so many things that need explaining to you
so that you can understand why I can't take your words
anymore.  If nothing else, I had hoped you would want to
sort things out at least so that the kids could see that we
could be together amicably.*

*It's sad that you feel it's embarrassing to see the kids. I never dreamt you were prepared to give them up so easily. It's your decision. You have to live with yourself, just like I have to. And I can live with myself because I never was a bad daughter. The fact that you will never know that is in your hands.*

*While you are not prepared to understand me and you, I do not want any contact with you whatsoever. I don't need a phone call from you while you still believe what you do about me. I'm cutting all ties because the ties you offer her are not worth anything. I am a human being, full of love and kindness, perhaps you'll say you've never seen it. Maybe you haven't. It baffles me that you don't want to know why you've never seen it. Maybe it's because you really believe I'm void of any decent feelings.*

*I hope one day you'll be able to read this letter as it is and not how you interpret it. Until that day, I fear we will never get the chance to have some kind of relationship. I doubt whether any daughter in the world would be as devoted as I have been in trying to sort out this mess. Now I give up my devotion to what has turned out to be a lost cause. At least I can sleep easy now.*

*I WILL ONLY EVER TAKE RESPONSIBILITY FOR MYSELF - NOT FOR YOU AS WELL.*

*Again, I'll leave you with the same as before,*

*I could have been your ever-loving daughter,*

*Georgia*

## CHAPTER FOURTEEN

# BEYOND THE UNTHINKABLE

Now Georgia was a daughter without a mother. And herself, a mother with two daughters. Could they possibly understand how this situation had come about? Or were they just going to assume that what had happened between her and her mother was normal? She had always hoped not telling them the truth would pay off in time to come. In any case, there was no way anyone would regard it as normal, would they?

Georgia was still upset and lost without her mother and needed some kind of confirmation that what had happened was understandable and went to see Janice for her assessment of it all. Her image of the best mother in the world had faded, but it still felt unnatural without Sylvie in her life.

"She's not fit to be a mother and should never have had a child" Janice said as Georgia soaked up her words in disbelief. 'So maybe I shouldn't have been born?' she thought to herself. 'I am the result of an unfit mother. But am I wrong? Did I still have to take the blame for me?' Without knowing what had made her mother think the way she did, did she still have to feel guilty of her own existence?' "I would have liked to know what made her the way she is. She's a narcissist." Janice said quietly as Georgia got up to leave. "I don't suppose anyone will ever know" Georgia replied. "I'm certainly not going to try and analyse me or her anymore. "I can't afford to. I'll just have to remember what you told me, put her in that imaginary box and throw it into a country that I'm never going to visit. It's time for me to end this misery. Thank you so much for your help" she said as she gestured a wave goodbye, *leaving the office along the same corridor and outside grounds. There was no squirrel this time.*

*So now it was pretty much official. Sylvie had been an unfit mother. OK. But Georgia was still getting these pangs of guilt erupting again and again. How could she possibly cast aside her own mother? How could she? Surely, she would be shunned by society. It couldn't be acceptable to the rest of the world, could it? Would she have to hang her head in shame for the choice she had made? Surely she would be an outcast, a daughter who didn't love her mother. What would people think of her? How would she be treated? She was going against the very person who gave her life. But she was in for a nice surprise.*

*Georgia had kept herself apart from all her father's relatives for some time now convincing herself that no one would want to keep in touch with her and hadn't bothered to make contact with anyone except one aunt, her father's sister, Rosie. Georgia had kept her up to date with all the family news including her mother and she was always genuinely concerned, but never taking sides. It was a relief to be able to tell her everything without any judgement.*

*Georgia's fear of rejection was now so massive and she didn't feel she could speak to her mother's family about what had occurred. It was complicated. A rift had broken out previously between Georgia and her mother's sister, Mary, when she had asked her to take a gift she had bought for her first cousin's wedding in the States. Mary and Mont were the only members of the family able to afford to go and Georgia thought her request was fair. But Mary refused point blank to take the gift and after Georgia told her mother about it, Sylvie took her sister's side. Before long, all of Sylvie's family had shut Georgia out. Even Mary and Mont's son Gary, had refused to meet up with her when he said on the phone one day "... because my mum says she won't babysit if I see you and we need a babysitter." She never spoke to or saw him again after that. Family never ceased to surprise her.*

*The girls showed no interest in seeing their grandmother and Georgia began to enjoy enormous comfort from responses of those around her and was gaining more and more confidence with the decision she had made to cut her mother out of her life. Months later she still had no cause to contact Sylvie and the lack of her mother's presence made her realise that she **was** getting on better without her. She had her family around her who made no demands on her emotionally and gave her their love unconditionally.*

*She comforted herself with her new appreciation of the things that really mattered. She had learned the hard way what her priorities in life were and no one could take them away now. She felt humbled to be allowed so much to appreciate. Her Larry, her girls, her life. She'd finally found the things most important to her. Nothing else mattered. Her survival was out of her hands but at least she had found what she had been searching for all her life. Now she could measure everything by her feelings. That was what counted. Whatever time she had left she was going to live it how she wanted. If anyone loved her then she knew it was because they accepted her for herself and how she wanted to be. As far as she was concerned, anyone who disliked her didn't know her. And those who chose not to know her were of no loss.*

*END OF ORIGINAL MANUSCRIPT*

## CHAPTER FIFTEEN

# JOINING THE NEW

Georgia had reached the end of the old manuscript and everything, including her, was so different now. She had used a portable typewriter back in the early 90's and now it was a laptop and she would have to re-type every word and her trusty dog-eared thesaurus was still around for this new part of the book.

The world was so different now, hardly recognisable in so many ways and not all good either. Mobile phones, computers, shops, streets, buildings, traffic, drivers, vehicles, people's attitudes, so-called experts, customer services, headline news, de-sensitised viewers at every turn, even the natural world had changed dramatically in the last 20 years due to pollution levels and bad management and now Covid 19. In fact, the only constant Georgia could see throughout these years had been her ever-growing passion to keep handwriting alive, always there in some shape or form for her to take up whenever she chose. Throughout all the turmoil and heartache, even when she was homeless, there was calligraphy work to be done and she was to devote the rest of her life to keeping handwriting alive.

Her profession as a calligrapher had started in 1987 when she was working as a legal secretary locally. Still the quiet mouse, she had braved the idea of re-writing her boss's filing cabinet labels with smart calligraphic Old English lettering, A-D, E-H, etc., while her boss was out to lunch and had just finished putting the last label in and returning to her own office, found a memo in the top of her typewriter. It read "This legal practice is now closed. Please remove your personal items and leave the building immediately. Signed "The Law Society." What? She looked around and noticed she was the only one in the small side office of three secretaries and ran into the corridor to see the firm's junior partner in the office opposite with his head in his hands, sobbing. Georgia's boss was the senior partner and it was October 19th, 1987 also known as Black Monday when the London Stock Market crashed, exposing the firm's client bank account and the money that he had embezzled. This was her first job back in the world of work after having the children. Sarah was eight and Sophie was five and they had both settled nicely into junior school. Georgia had enjoyed her small taste of independence and undeterred, began to look the next day for work by signing up with a local employment agency. They found her a two-week assignment in a firm of local solicitors and on the first morning there, as she flicked through the file at the top of the pile, she realised she was dealing with the married couple who were suing her old boss, as their house purchase deposit of £60K had found its way onto the London Stock Market. What a small world. Her heart wasn't in this kind of work and she continued looking for something that fitted in with school time and found herself thinking more and more about calligraphy as an unusual means of earning a living.

She had taught herself how to use the specially-shaped nibs and had done plenty of calligraphy for friends and family, making table plans for weddings, anniversaries and inscribing place cards, poems and pros and decided to put an ad in the classified column of the local newspaper, advertising her skill as 'Calligrapher - No job too big or too small,' and waited. It took three months before she had a response.

The first enquiry was from a Mr Dunhill and she was sure someone was playing a trick on her as she smoked Dunhill cigarettes. It was too much of a coincidence. It turned out that Mr Dunhill's enquiry was indeed genuine. His son was getting barmitzvar'd in a few months' time and needed "everything done in calligraphy." It was to be wonderful work experience for Georgia. She still has the picture of the Barmitzvah boy that his father had sent her on the day, standing by the football table plan she had made. Against all doubters, mainly her own, the business started to grow. She was being contacted by famous names, foreign dignitaries, the aristocracy, all enquiring about her calligraphy. The work was coming in so fast that she advertised for help and from the hundreds of applicants she found 2 wonderful calligraphers who lived locally and used them as and when the work was too much for her to do alone. This was a new beginning. Knowing it was important to keep handwriting alive, she bought two second-hand desks, some cupboards and converted the dining room into an office.

By 1994, the work was coming in from some very big names, including Chanel, British Olympic Association, Sir Richard Attenborough Associates, Lord Alan Sugar, Mont Blanc, Mandarin Oriental Hotel Group and Georgia had just landed a contract with WH Smith, all because of a request from a lady to write some place cards for her daughter's wedding. As the mother of the bride-to-be laid the WHS place cards on her desk, Georgia thought 'If WHS customers are coming to me then WHS needs to offer my services to their customers!' The Head of Stationery at WHS' Head Office in Swindon agreed to run a pilot Calligraphy Service in five of their top selling wedding stationery branches. She had said 'no one *anywhere in the world* had ever offered such a service in the retail sector'. Georgia had hit the big time and went on to meet Head of Stationery at M&S at his office in Baker Street. He liked the idea too and she set to creating and designing the first easy-to-order retail calligraphy service and was immersed in everything to do with merchandising, point of sale material and general retail transactions.

It was fortunate that in the previous year, she had set up the calligraphy service as a business based on what the London East Training Enterprise Scheme had taught her. They offered new businesses help with set up costs and advice, all for free. She learnt how to keep accounting books, market the business, what mark-up, gross margins, turnover, net profit and loss really meant and was fascinated to learn about strengths and weaknesses of a business. There were charts, statistics, cash flow forecasts, lectures, hands-on help just by calling experts if needed, real experts who had experience of running their own successful companies and she loved being a part of this world of commerce. Thank you LETEC.

But work had become stressful and this was where, despite business being successful, Georgia's emotional weakness had taken its toll as she lay in the hospital bed waiting for the craniotomy. Larry had walked in waving a large piece of paper, smiling. It was her first order from WHS. She was elated and knew she could delegate the work to one of her team. The order was processed, completed and the account was settled in due course, so everything was fine.

Friends Pip and Keith had helped build the pond a couple of years earlier. Chatting one afternoon in the garden, they had all agreed the holly tree needed to come down and a new water feature would improve the empty and boring lawned garden. Georgia and Pip laughed as they watched Keith and Larry, sitting cross-legged either side of the tree each holding a handle of the long saw, "They're like chalk and cheese," Pip had said. Keith was slim and tall, Larry was short and stocky and they agreed it was like watching Laurel & Hardy in action. How they laughed.

The pond became Georgia's road to recovery after the operation and she used to sit for hours discovering the natural life below and above the water she never knew existed. She saw her first newt, some frogspawn and watched a heron overlook the fish from the lofty height of the shed roof. So much life, all from her pond. One day she was so mesmerised at what she was watching, she had ignored the heavy rain that day, happily sitting underneath an old golfing umbrella in her anorak until it was time to go in and, closing the umbrella and, covering her head with the hood, discovered the rain had been dripping in it for hours as it drenched her. Walking into the house completely soaked, she thought it was hilarious. It was the last thing she expected considering she had stayed dry all day out there, but she felt so glad to be alive and saw the funny side, at last.

In all the chaos of the recent past Georgia had lost her priorities and confidence in anything remotely connected to her personal life but the pond helped her regain her appreciation of nature. With all its beauty she began to realise everything important to her was being slowly restored, not changed and she started to see what her priorities were again. Looking after her children, keeping them safe, providing for her family, being the good wife. But the last one wasn't so easy to do.

She was discussing the new kitchen wall colour with the new builder, Dougie, when she gasped, not believing what had just occurred. She recognised the pain instantly. Dougie moved forward to steady her as she staggered forward. 'Another haemorrhage? No, surely not.' Her mind tried to make sense of the pain in her head, in the same place as eight months earlier. Was this part of the healing process? Or maybe she was making more of it than she should? Or was she finally getting her comeuppance? Memories of her mother had faded into almost oblivion but had suddenly jumped into her mind and the familiar 'guilty Georgia' was back in an instant.

It was like Groundhog Day. Larry was driving her back to the hospital in the car, taking the same route he knew so well. Neither of them could believe it. This was surreal and she must be mistaken. The doctors will confirm it as soon as they get there. It couldn't possibly be a second haemorrhage. The neurosurgeon had told her how the operation had been a complete success. There was no further treatment needed and no future problems expected.

Still conscious and walking into A&E, Larry explained to the receptionist what had happened as Georgia sat nearby, still in shock. Within moments, not even minutes, she was promptly taken to the now familiar scanning department down in the bowels of the Royal London.

Back in the A&E cubicle, waiting for the results of the scan, Larry told her he "couldn't go through this again." The thought was distressing him already. He had been so supportive there by her side all those months ago. She hadn't given much thought to the anxieties and trauma he must have gone through. He had described a kind of shell-shock he'd felt just before she had had the craniotomy. He had held himself together, being the strong one for all of them, and the pieces were only just starting to come together again now. Surely this was a false alarm.

They both recognised the registrar as he walked along the corridor towards them. He recognised them too but failed to smile as he reached the bed, "I'm sorry, it is another haemorrhage," he said as he showed them the scan result. There was no denying the now familiar blob on the right-hand temporal lobe. In fact it was in exactly the same place as before. "How can that be?" Larry asked. "We were told Georgia would have no problems after the operation. I don't understand."

"There appears to be some residue that was left after the first craniotomy. It is very rare but it shouldn't be a problem. All we have to do is perform the same procedure all over again."

"Another craniotomy?" she stuttered. With all those risks again? She watched Larry's face as the colour began to drain away. But Georgia had already gone into her 'pre-op mode,' "What will be will be" she said to Larry, resigning herself to what she knew was coming. This time her concern was for Larry. He had already proved his devotion but was this going to be too much for him to bear?

It was like watching an old movie, back in the same trauma ward, waving to some of the now familiar nurses as she entered by wheelchair. Again, she felt a fraud. The pain wasn't too bad at all now and she was being given even more attention than the first time. Larry arranged his bed of chairs next to hers. He must have found some kind of inner strength as they watched their future unfold, again.

As the operation day approached after two weeks of lying flat again, Georgia was becoming increasingly more philosophical. There was absolutely no point in worrying. It would be utterly futile. If she was to survive this then she would be in whatever condition it was to be. And if she died, then so be it.

## CHAPTER SIXTEEN

# UNHAPPY FAMILIES

Georgia recovered miraculously intact again from the second haemorrhage and subsequent second craniotomy and the family settled back into a normality of sorts. She chose to ignore the idea that she could have another haemorrhage at any time, realising this was no way to live and that she had to take advantage of every extra minute she had been given and not waste a moment. Her life began to feel precious and fragile.

In 1997, they took a family holiday to Venice. It was a pleasant enough time for them all. Larry was still terribly over-protective of Georgia and she was beginning to feel stifled, controlled even. She couldn't ignore the recent discovery that life was too short to waste and she found herself pulling away from him more and more, full of guilt at her inadequacies and fearful of her ever-growing discontentment with him. She was afraid the truth would come tumbling out of her mouth one day. The truth that although she had tried so desperately to learn to love him, it never came. She knew she couldn't keep it to herself much longer. She'd had such high hopes for them. She so wanted them to be the solid couple she yearned for but knew after 19 years of marriage, that day was never going to happen. Maybe she wasn't capable of loving anyone but her children and was terrified at the thought of telling him so. It was as the morning light came through the bedroom window one day, unplanned she quietly and most unexpectedly opened her eyes, turned to Larry and said "'I'm sorry, I can't stay married to you anymore. I don't love you." She had pushed it aside for so long but at this precise moment she was no longer afraid to tell the truth. And for the first time, Larry's reaction didn't matter anymore. She had dreaded coming clean, expecting him to physically lash out at her, possibly even killing her. But it didn't matter now. She had confessed the truth and there was nothing more to say. She had no thoughts of future plans, no arrangements, no support, no nothing but she just had to say the words. 'Oh god' she thought, 'at last, I've said it. I can breathe,' feeling the weight lift from her shoulders as if by magic.

Larry didn't hurt or kill her. He did lash out verbally, at which he was expert. Being verbally aggressive was symptomatic of a Napoleonic complex. He was always the one to shout and she was always, until now, the submissive one. He was devastated and so too were the girls. There was no easy way to explain that their entire world of family was about to change into something unknown to them. She knew the pain they were feeling and was so very sorry to do this to everyone. Larry's sister had just given birth to her first child and their one visit to the hospital was the last time Georgia was to see the child or any of Larry's family again. Family, friends, everyone she had known for years suddenly vanished. The divorce was protracted and contained a viciousness she had come to expect from Larry. But all that mattered to her now were the practicalities. She wanted nothing from Larry. She wanted nothing from anyone except the freedom to be herself and care for her children. There was a financial settlement of £5,000 after clearing the mortgage arrears, which was to be the deposit for the two-bedroomed flat for the girls and her. Larry had reluctantly moved into his sister's empty house that she was now renting to him. The future seemed hazy but she was so relieved to have lost the heavy weight she had carried on her shoulders for so many years that Georgia didn't see any major problems ahead. Except that Larry had told her some weeks later, grinning with revengeful pleasure, that he had told the girls about the 'fling' she had had some ten years earlier. It was during the days when she sat for hours in the armchair, just staring. They had moved house and had employed a builder to complete some renovations. The tall, strong and good-looking builder came on to Georgia and, thinking it might be an escape route to her misery at the time, had accepted his advances, just once. It was to be a very short and regrettable 'fling.' Georgia had become friends with the neighbour who lived in the house opposite and after both of them confiding in their infidelities, their friendship grew, often 'popping in for a cuppa' every now and then. The woman knocked on Georgia's door one afternoon saying "I need to speak to you." Georgia said "Come in. Larry's here if you don't mind talking in front of him. I have told him about your situation" trying to deflect Georgia's own guilt, but he can keep a secret. He won't tell a soul, I promise." What Georgia didn't know was that Larry was behind her as the woman said 'Oh, so Larry knows about you having the fling with the builder then?" Hell broke out that day and after much emotional turmoil and arguments, Larry said he would forgive her and would never discuss it again. But there were always his occasional intimidatory remarks alluding to the incident, which Georgia chose to accept as her 'punishment.'

## CHAPTER SEVENTEEN

# EXPECT THE UNEXPECTED

Sometimes we take the knowledge we have gained for granted. At least that's what Georgia did when the mortgage broker told her he was having a small problem finding her a mortgage because of her past joint-arrears and suggested, as she had a buyer in place, she should exchange contracts on your house and "by the time the completion date comes, I will have found you a mortgage for the flat. Then you can complete the house sale and flat purchase all on the same day." As an experienced conveyancing secretary, Georgia knew this was common practice and had witnessed the procedure many times before, so she exchanged contracts on the matrimonial house and waited for the mortgage offer to appear. But it never did and nor did A J, the so-called mortgage broker who vanished off the face of the earth days before she was due to complete the purchase. He was simply nowhere to be found and nor was the mortgage offer he had promised.

After holding out to the last moment and praying that the broker would save the day and appear with the offer, she realised her and the girls actually had nowhere to go. It was now 12 noon on moving day and they were supposed to be moving to the 2 bed flat now. Outside was the large removal lorry and a charity lorry too, already filled with the wanted and unwanted furniture and household items. As the day unfolded, thinking on her feet, she stalled the drivers for extra time, grabbing some bags of clothes just as they had finished loading, realising the rest might have to be in storage for some time.

Now the lorries were filled and sent on their way, one to the charity shop, that was easy. The one with all their worldly goods had to go into storage until she had found somewhere for her and the girls to live. Ok, so that was the furniture sorted out but what about the girls? Oh, and the dog! There was only one thing she could do and that was to call Larry. He knew the sale of the house was happening today and after explaining the situation to him quickly, she asked if he could take the girls until she found somewhere for them to live. He was there within five minutes and then they were all gone. She was alone as she handed over the house keys to the new owners of their beautiful detached house and her pond. She now had just one key in her possession, for the car and she was homeless.

Sally and Syd, were lovely neighbours just two doors away and came to Georgia's rescue when she knocked on their door, putting her up for two days while she called her good friend Ivy in Southend. She too was happy to help, offering her a place to stay for as long as she needed.

Ivy had recently been widowed, although to Georgia's surprise, she was elated to find herself free of the "pig of a man," as she called him. Ivy was learning the Southend knowledge with the intention of becoming a local cab driver and took Georgia along to join the classes for a few weeks while she stayed with her. But she was having to go back every other day, looking for a suitable place for the girls and her to live. She spent some nights in the car rather than keep driving back and forth. Money was tight and she withdrew the £500 Larry and her had in a savings account, which later he said he would never forgive her for taking, to pay for petrol and food. She was in Southend for 6 weeks before contacting another good friend in Walthamstow, who also offered her a place to stay whenever she wanted.

So Georgia moved to Walthamstow for 3 weeks before finally finding a place above a shop back in Ilford. She showed it to the girls before she signed the rental agreement. They loved it. It was in the High Street, very familiar to them and close to their friends. They were so happy to be there and she was glad to have her kids back again.

She felt she was coping ok with the girls now. They were typical teenagers, moody and formidable and their lives were like a rollercoaster at times, with new friends, ideas, attitudes, jobs and boyfriends for them all. Sarah was now nineteen and Sophie was sixteen when about 8pm one evening Georgia answered a knock at the door. It was Ivy from Southend. "Get your shoes on, girl" she said to a dazed Georgia, literally dragging her (she hadn't even changed) to an 'over 30's singles' night somewhere in Essex. This was her first venture into the single scene which she had no interest in anyway. She had been content in the knowledge she had divorced Larry for the right reasons, because she didn't love him and not because there was someone else waiting in the wings for her. She had made a decision to end the marriage and she did not want to find someone else. Reluctantly she got in Ivy's car and feeling awkward and alien in this large hall, she did notice a good-looking guy standing by the dance floor with his friend holding their drinks and before she knew what had happened, he had asked her to dance and they started dating. Her, dating after all these years? What a very strange thing to do at forty-four!

## CHAPTER EIGHTEEN

# TWINKLE TOES

Georgia was still running the calligraphy business and very reluctantly bought her first computer. Reluctantly due to the nature of the business, handwriting, that is. The years of experience in admin, secretarial duties, LETEC's help and the I.T. classes she'd taken after the divorce had paid off. Plus the GNVQ on desktop publishing, data protection and copyright law, she was now creating her own terms and conditions, logos, invoices and just about everything she needed for the business. It was important she had a corporate image for the business. This was the only way she felt people could take what she was doing seriously. Was she the only one selling calligraphy? It sure felt like it and it wasn't long before the work dried up. Computers replaced handwriting now and she had to go back to legal work.

Ironically, the computer, sitting on the table by the window was to become a great consolation and asset despite how she was dedicating so much time to avoid computers whenever possible. And then, the madness of dating a man at her age was full of so many impracticalities. After all, she was the mother of two daughters. And he was far too young for her at just thirty-two. What kind of example was she setting? Sarah had already commented the morning after she'd heard the headboard knock in the bedroom next door to hers. Georgia remembered it wasn't right from her own experiences with her mother. The relationship with Paul lasted two years. He had asked her to move in with him but she didn't feel the girls were ready for her to leave and she didn't see a future with him anyway. A partner was not a priority. Putting food on the table and keeping her girls warm was.

So while the girls were out in the evenings, the computer became Georgia's source of social life. She joined Freeserve online chat and entered a world of rooms for twenties, thirties, forties and silver surfers. Ever compliant, at forty-four she never veered from the forties Room, although she was often approached by what she can only assume were men in their twenties and even teens. For the first time she was learning, from the safety of her own home, all about sex. Wow. What a revelation. It was wonderful for someone who had been so innocent, to discover how men thought. It was one of the greatest learning curves she'd ever had and considered 'one day, I'll write a book about my adventures during these days.'

One evening, Georgia and a girlfriend joined a new salsa group which took her away from the computer once a week. She'd made quite a few new single friends there, male and female, including Viv who, after telling her about her current situation at home, said she would be happy to rent her a room in her house for a while. The idea of leaving home? Georgia? She came home and sat the girls down and talked about it. They were keen for her to leave. Sarah now twenty-three and Sophie twenty, were now both working full-time and Georgia knew they could afford to live in the flat without her. It seemed to make sense to move out and for them to stay. There was no reason not to give it a try and they agreed to have a trial run for three months to see if they could manage the place by themselves. They did and seemed very happy with the arrangement although Georgia was still very conscious of not abandoning or neglecting them, mindful of her mother and her, and decided Enfield was a little too far away and moved into another friend Lori's property in Chadwell Heath, just a couple of miles from Ilford. Lori was older than Georgia and had got married a year earlier and rented out her flat which had now come up for renewal, except the tenant no longer needed to rent it anymore. So Georgia moved into Lori's pretty little one-bedroomed flat and life seemed to be on the up, at last. But the girls were using more and more avoidance tactics, hardly ever coming to visit and rarely making contact. She knew they had their own lives but there was an air of hostility about them. They still seemed angry with her, even though she thought moving out would solve the problem. It didn't.

Georgia found renting expensive and, having a reasonably well-paid job as a legal secretary again, decided to start looking for a place to buy and after carefully checking the girls were still happy with their living arrangement, the girls were increasingly hostile towards her. When she questioned them, their responses didn't make sense. One reason Sarah gave was that "after you arranged to play a game of squash with me after work one evening, I told you I had forgotten to take my trainers to work with me and you were evil." Georgia admitted she was disappointed that they weren't going to play squash together because she didn't have her trainers and that Sarah didn't want to go home to get them first. She hadn't seen her in weeks and was so looking forward to catching up with her, but she wasn't 'evil.'

And one of Sophie's responses to Georgia's question "Why are you being so hateful towards me?" was responded with "When you noticed the smell of gas coming from outside our new flat and you insisted I contact the gas board to check everything was safe", "Yes," Georgia said as she continued, saying how she hated the idea of her mother not being there when the gas man would arrive as she thought he might be dangerous. Georgia assured her this was standard practice and there was nothing to worry about and promised to call her that evening to make sure everything was ok. Except, Georgia fell asleep after dinner that evening and didn't wake up until she heard the phone ring, well past eleven o'clock and was given a blasting of "I could have been raped and left in a ditch somewhere!" Another reason for her contempt for her mother now was, she said, when she was starting a new job and had been invited to the firm's Christmas party. Sophie had met all the staff she would be working with there. Apparently, she had struck up a conversation with two of the girls in the office who asked what was in her drink. She had offered them a taste which they declined and she later heard them speaking about her in the ladies' toilets a short time afterwards, which she said she found very upsetting. Georgia asked if she had said anything to upset them and was told "That's typical of you. Siding with strangers!" What did she say that was so wrong? Nothing was making any sense.

Georgia bought and moved into a one-bedroom flat just a few miles from the girls who also decided to buy a flat between the two of them, just a mile from the flat they had been renting with and after Georgia had moved out.

Georgia arranged the day of the move for the girls, which developed into the worst moving day of all time.

## CHAPTER NINETEEN

# WORST MOVE EVER

Curtis, the one man and his van had easily moved Georgia's bed and a few items from the flat in Ilford to her new apartment a couple of miles away and knew she could rely on him for the girls move now. She had left most of the furniture with them and he said he would bring a much larger van this time. They were all expecting a quick move to the girl's new apartment, just a couple of minutes away.

At 9.30am Curtis arrived as they were organising boxes and bags, all labelled and ready to load. He said it was best to load the big stuff like the sofa and fridge and beds first and so they waited for his friend Peter who was due to arrive "any minute now."

With the boxes and bags ready, they all waited for Curtis' pal Peter, while they stared at the huge contents of their new home now outside in the open air on the balcony at the top of the concrete stairs. They all knew it would be impossible for any of them to lift the heavy furniture down the very steep steps into the van below. It needed Curtis and his friend. It was 10.30am when Curtis tried calling Peter but there was no reply. Waiting patiently, there was plenty to keep them occupied, opening boxes, searching for 'stuff' and then sealing them up again. Then there was a glimmer of hope when Peter answered the phone around 2pm saying he would be delayed a couple of hours, without explanation. So they all tried to relax and waited some more. Somehow the hours passed without much notice when Georgia realised she could reduce some items the girls had suddenly today decided not to take with by running to every charity shop down in the

High Street, trying to get them to take the excess furniture. But she had no luck. It was too short notice for them.

Peter finally turned up at **9pm** that evening. It was dark outside when he explained the reason for such a long delay. His daughter had been arrested for smuggling drugs of some kind and he had to stay with her at court all day. He arrived suited and booted, hardly ready to load furniture but move the furniture, he and Curtis finally did. The move was worsened by the fact that they didn't get to *unload* the van at the new place until way past 11pm, which meant the girls' new neighbours were far from happy with the noise the furniture and metal objects were making as they banged and clanged along the communal railings up the stairs to their first-floor apartment. People were coming out of their front doors, complaining and moaning and at one point, no one could get up or down the stairs with so much 'stuff' in the way and the girls never actually got to see their neighbours until after that night. It was past midnight before Curtis and Peter were gone and everyone was exhausted and stressed to the hilt.

Unbeknown to the girls, Georgia was having problems in the solicitor's office where she worked. She was being bullied by the three other secretaries in her office, all because she happened to mention she was friends with her now boss's wife, unaware that one of the secretaries had had an affair with him. She felt the shutters come down the day she mentioned the wife's name and was treated to what she now knows as bullying in the workplace. She regularly ran into the local church at lunchtime where she cried in private and was physically and emotionally drained most evenings by the time she got home. The girls never knew about this and when they had told Georgia that they were buying a place of their own together, they naturally expected her to process the conveyancing legalities for them. Giving them some feeble excuse about being too busy at work, Georgia hadn't actually been at the office for over a month because she was so depressed.

But the thing that really puzzled Georgia that day back waiting to move was that the girls had told her they had got their mortgage from AJ, the mortgage broker. What? How could they? She had had a nightmare move because he had disappeared without a mortgage offer. She had told them never to deal with him after what he had done eight years earlier, leaving them homeless. Had they simply ignored her plea. Why? Was there a connection with her ex-brother-in-law's letting agency where Sophie was now working? Was this a conspiracy? Or was she just paranoid like the girls said she was?

It was difficult for Georgia to cope with the bullying but did not tell the girls and tried to keep things light between them. Calling round unexpectedly to see them in their new apartment she was looking forward to catching up with their news. It had been a while since they had been together. It was around 6pm and Sarah was on her way home from work when Sophie opened the door and let Georgia in without saying a word, going back to the living room continuing to eat her dinner from a tray on her lap. Georgia sat on the armchair and starting to chat "How are you? Are you settled?" Sophie said "Be quiet." Georgia said "Pardon?"

Sophie barked "If you can't be quiet, wait in the car until Sarah gets in." She knows now she should have tipped the food over Sophie's head just then but the old, quiet Georgia mouse just walked out and went home, never to set foot in the flat again.

Georgia couldn't cope with how the girls were treating her and called Larry to see if he could shed any light on why they were being so aggressive towards her. Inviting himself over, Georgia saw his eyes scan the rooms leading off the small hallway as he walked in. Georgia showed him into the bright and welcoming lounge and they continued their conversation, coming to no conclusions until Larry suggested they all meet. "Ok" she said as she got up to show him out, asking him to "arrange it with them, anytime, anywhere." Still seated, he asked for a glass of water and sat thoughtfully, grinning at her for ages before she had to ask him again to go. She could see his control now but it didn't work on her anymore.

Larry arrived again a few days later, this time with Sarah and Sophie and Georgia couldn't help notice how they had arranged the dining chairs with the three of them sitting facing her one chair. Then interrogation began, "You said….!" and "I said…" and "I hate you!" ensued. Georgia had lived without the screaming and shouting now for some time and suddenly saw this smokescreen. They had not said anything factual. They were like wild animals on the attack and the more she tried to find out what they were referring to, the more vague and aggressive they became. It was obvious that she was not going to get to the bottom of this while all three of them were being so unreasonable. Georgia started to cry as the hour-long onslaught waned. Larry and the girls left the flat, never to return.

The personal tragedy about to enter Georgia's world was unexpected, to say the least. It was, as they say, a 'slow burn' but hitting much too hard on impact. The impact being the point of realisation which she hadn't noticed creeping up on her for more than a year now. The girls no longer wanted to see her. They had used odd excuses and absurd reasons for cancelling meeting their mother, The Sunday lunch she had made for them was thrown away and they hadn't even bother to explain their absence and concerned that they may have had an accident on the way to her, she called Sarah's mobile and all she could hear was her contempt. It took her breath away. What was going on? Was it this P.A.S, Parental Alienation Syndrome she had heard of? It was probably because Larry had told them about the fling she had had. Her girls were certainly alienating themselves and for a while, but would they hate her so much that they refused to talk or meet with her? Ok, she wasn't a perfect mother, she knew that but had little to go on. She was aware she had overcompensated for the divorce and gave the girls free reign to do as they pleased. Georgia's philosophy then was that she trusted their judgement over hers and was sure they would make the right decisions in life. More so than she was capable of, she thought. Georgia now had the feeling that the girls may never forgive her, for whatever reason, for the rest of her life.

Georgia rarely spoke with Larry these days except on rare occasions when Georgia felt she had no choice but to ask him how the girls were because they never answered her calls. There was the time when he told her Sophie had moved to a new address, withholding the details. Within an hour Georgia received a text from Sophie "I know Dad told you where I live. Do not attempt to visit the area." Georgia was speechless.

It was some time after the girls first showed no interest in restoring their relationship and certainly not wanting to enter into any positive dialogue that Georgia was beginning to despair at not having contact with them and again, called Larry to ask how they were. He answered "I'm not supposed to talk to you. Ask them yourself" and then hung up.

As capable as Georgia was in everything practical, it was no surprise to discover her past experiences had left her with a massive fear of rejection and once she realised the girls would have nothing to do with her, her fear grew and it became impossible to do more than send them an email or a text every so often, asking them to meet her so they could talk and sort everything out. But the few responses they did make were so full of hatred that she reduced contact to every few months, when they responded independently with nothing but vicious retorts, cutting and pasting some of her words back to her, adding more contempt here and there. Nothing made any sense again. This was a living nightmare.

Her mind raced, trying to distract herself from the possibility that her children would no longer be in her life. She was on her way home from work, another day of bullying, driving as usual along the long, straight forest road that led to the small lane where she lived, so easy to miss if you don't know where you're going.  How could she live without her children? She couldn't.  The thought was unbearable.  The thought of living was unbearable as she took a deep breath, putting her right foot on the accelerator, letting go of the steering wheel and closing her eyes. 'Let me die,' she prayed as she instinctively opening them again, concerned for the car heading towards her. 'I can't even do that' as she slowed the car to 50mph.

When she got home she opened the laptop, typed in 'suicide' and waited.  Google's choices were more than she had expected and she clicked on one that looked official.  Reading down the words of comfort she read 'We can help you during this time' and was prompted to click the 'OPEN HERE" button.  The screen went black.  Completely black for what seemed like an eternity although it was probably just a minute.  Then the screen changed back into words of comfort, saying 'Sometimes we need a moment of calm to help us feel a little better.' It was right.  She did feel better.  The feeling to end it all had passed.  It hadn't change anything though.

Working at the solicitor's office was now almost impossible, even after confiding in the office manager about the bullying, she knew no one was going to deal with this problem in her favour and releasing the tension in the church down the road from the office at lunchtime was now her only salvation.  Often she would sit in the most hidden part of the building to cry. 'These are small town women with small town minds,' she thought as she pictured how they huddled together in the office, giggling and whispering incessantly.

She had forgotten about the old friend who had introduced her to a newly divorced woman that was looking for a single friend to go out with. Georgia had told Amy about the bullying at work and she had asked Georgia for her CV, saying she would pass it to her HR department and if there were any vacancies, someone would be in touch.

## CHAPTER TWENTY

# CRISIS AT CHRISTMAS

Georgia knew this first Christmas without the girls was going to be unbearable but what could she do? Feeling so worthless, she had already cut herself off from her friends and as all contact with her mother's family had stopped, she didn't believe any family on her father's side would want to know her now either. This was a 'happy families' time of year, something she'd never enjoyed. She had to find somewhere to lose herself. Tony was with his parents and their relationship was too new to share this time of year with them. 'There must be people less fortunate than me. I must be of some help to someone' she thought.

She found CRISIS on the internet and signed up as a volunteer helper for Christmas and Boxing Day at a homeless shelter in London, glad to have something to take her mind off everything that was surrounding her. At a secret location only given to her on Christmas Eve the event was in London's King's Cross area and parking her car outside a large empty-looking building, Georgia gave her name to the official man at the front door and was handed a white plastic badge with "CRISIS 2009" printed in black. The doorman handed her a blue marker pen and asked her to write her name on it and she proceeded to enter an unknown world which, surprisingly proved to be much nicer than the one she had just left back home. There were hundreds of people inside. There were so many it was difficult to work out which people were the homeless ones. There were people wandering around, some preparing food, people cleaning toilets and others just sitting chatting together.

Georgia had completed a hairdressing course at her local college when the girls were very young. At that time, she thought it was a good idea to learn how to cut their fringes in a straight line instead of taking them to the hairdressers every couple of weeks and as she was leaving for CRISIS that morning, she had grabbed her scissors and comb, thinking 'just in case any of the homeless people need a haircut.'

After spending a few minutes checking out the activities listed on a wall, she approached one of the organisers and said "I have brought my hairdressing scissors with me. Would anyone like a haircut?" and was immediately whisked away to another section of the building where she saw some people were having showers and being given towels and fresh clothes to wear. There was a dentist and a chiropodist. Suddenly there were so many more things provided for the homeless people than she could have ever imagined. There was a woman standing with an empty chair in front of her and a queue of men waiting for haircuts. Georgia grabbed another chair and called to the queue "Next!" She went home exhausted after cutting at least 150 heads of hair but what an experience! Tomorrow was to be a repeat of today.

## CHAPTER TWENTY-ONE

# HIDDEN DEPTHS

Georgia rarely socialised these days, only chatting online now. It was low risk. Low risk of rejection. She had become almost hermit-like when she received a message from a dating site she had joined some years earlier. She was used to chatting online with men and Tony and her had clicked on the site thanks to their profiles sharing a mutual love of music and when Georgia asked him for his number, she made that first ever call to a stranger and his voice was wonderful to her ears. It was soft and soothing, unscripted and relaxed. He made her laugh when he told her about how his kitchen door had come off its hinges and that he now slept with it in his bedroom. He made Georgia laugh. What a thing to do. They asked each other lots of questions and quickly got around to the subject of music. Had she heard of Steely Dan? Georgia replied so fast with "Yeah! With Donald Fagen! I've got the Nightfly album and what about Santana and The Eagles?" With their mutual love of music established they continued to talk for hours, like they had been best friends for years and arranged to meet the following evening in the pub near Georgia's flat. On that first date she told him about her situation with her girls. He couldn't understand it and it pleased her when he said 'I'm so sorry. I can't relate to such an awful experience.' He lived locally, was also divorced and she admired the dedication he had to his own daughters, insisting on seeing them regularly. She got to thinking how lucky they were that their dad was so devoted, wanting to see them, unlike her own father.

Rarely, going on a blind date just to stave off boredom, Georgia would have never let her date know where she lived and was ready to walk home alone that night. But it was snowing and cold and although it was just a short walk home, she was happy to let Tony drive her back with just a "Goodnight" peck on the cheek. "I love your personality Tony. I know it sounds corny but I mean this... I really hope we can stay friends." Tony replied, "I want more than just friendship. I want a proper relationship." She had met quite a few men from the internet over the past few years and knew the experiences she had had could never amount to anything long-lasting. No one would want a serious relationship with her and her issues. She'd been on her own for 11 years and had only met men to keep her mind off of her own situation at home. A proper relationship with her was unthinkable. But Tony was different. He was a genuine guy.

It took Tony a while to get used to the occasional chats Georgia had with her dear friend Joe on the phone, usually late at night. She'd met Joe in her teens and they had kept in touch all these years. They had had similar problems as children and despite their individual ups, downs, marriages and divorces, they had always managed to keep their friendship alive. He'd had a problem mother, as his eulogy in 2015 stated, "Joe had a difficult start in life". Joe was always just a phone call away whenever a crisis loomed. It wasn't until they were both in their 50's before Georgia realised just how much they had in common. So much was becoming clearer now. She was the pupil and he was always the old soul Buddhist, philosophical, rational and reasonable. He believed in fair play and always fought for the underdog.

It was 2009 when Joe helped her make a big discovery about her father when during one of their regular evening chats analysing their own parents, she made the throw-away comment, "I hate my father".

"Why?" he said.

"Because he just left. He didn't want me and he didn't care about me anymore after the divorce. I didn't even know if he would make it to the wedding. The only time I saw him was when I went to him. He never called, he never tried to see me. He never made any arrangements where I was concerned. He made a new life for himself and Rita and her daughter, then Scott arrived and he just forgot about me."

Joe interrupted, "But how do you KNOW that? Maybe he wasn't allowed to see you."

"What do you mean?" she said.

"Well, how do you know someone wasn't stopping your father from seeing you?"

"What, like my mother, you mean?"

"Yes" he said.

"Sadly, I'll never know. He's gone, I can't ask him now," she said, closing the subject.

But days later, she couldn't help thinking about the idea. Was it possible? Could her mother have imposed such an order on her father? She would never know. Or could she? Tom had died 26 years ago but his common-law-wife

Rita, was still alive. Georgia's great aunt was still in touch with Scott, her half-brother. He was still part of the family. Georgia had gone to his wedding some years earlier but rarely kept in touch, only seeing him at occasional family gatherings. He lived in Surrey, so far away from her world. Now she was regretting not keeping in touch and decided to call his mother and ask the question Joe had posed.

She knew Rita's voice well. After all, she had been her mother's best friend for some years. It used to be a strong and confident voice, but now she answered the phone sounding somewhat weaker than she had remembered. It only took her saying "It's Georgia" before Rita knew exactly who she was and seemed happy to hear from her. They chatted for short while before Rita told her that, apart from the hand injury she had sustained during the car crash when Tom had died, she was now very sick and couldn't talk for long. Suffering shortness of breath and waiting for hospital treatment, she had to take regular rest. Not wanting to keep her, Georgia started, "Look Rita, I know this is going to sound very odd and you don't have to give me an answer, but if you can I'd just like to know the truth, whatever that is, if you know it. Please don't worry about hurting my feelings. It's just the truth that I'm after if you know it. You see, I never saw much of my father after he and my mum got divorced and I was wondering whether my mother stopped my father from seeing me. Do you know if she did?" holding her breath and waiting. Without any hesitation, Rita replied "Oh yes! I am 100% positive your mother stopped your father from seeing you. I don't know what the hold was that she had over him but I know he was always upset at not being able to see you. He would never discuss it." She continued that her own daughter had once called him "daddy" and he was mad at her and said "No one calls me daddy except my Georgia!" Georgia was stunned. Her father loved her. He loved her. He didn't want to exclude her from his life and she never knew, for all these years She was now 55 and had just found out her father loved her. Her father had always loved her.

Suddenly, the image of Tom sobbing on the stairs all those years ago was in her head. Is that WHEN it happened? Had her mother laid down her rules to him THAT day? The day Georgia knew something terrible had just happened and was too scared to come in and instead, had taken her bike to the park and came home later to find he was gone, never to come back. Had her mother THAT much power over him? Or was he just weak? What hold could she have had over him? Was it sex? They had often met after the divorce, always in his car with Georgia in the back seat, pretending to be asleep so as not to get in the way. She was far too young and innocent to know what those movements her mother was making as she leaned towards him in the front bench seat and what was she was doing with her hands? And the heavy breathing? Now she was an adult and had a pretty good idea what that hold on him was. Was he so weak-willed to accept those terms? Just cheap thrills in a car as long as he didn't contact his daughter?

## CHAPTER TWENTY-TWO

# THE PURPOSE

Expecting only rejection at every turn now, Georgia was delighted and surprised to receive any approval as well as confirmation about her decision to disown Sylvie. A distant aunt on her father's side was quick to agree with the many observations Georgia had made about her mother. Georgia's parents were second cousins, so both families had been aware of each other even before they were married. Although her own memory was clouded by time, this aunt could remember occasions that had convinced her years ago that Sylvie's behaviour was, at the very least, "questionable."

It was a small wedding in the local Registrar Office in Barking and Georgia and Tony were very happy for the low-key event with just immediate family, except of course, Georgia's children were missing. She had invited them but with no response, described the day as "bitter sweet." Joe and her great aunt were there and with Tony's parents and girls, they celebrated the day with lunch at the local Italian restaurant.

Tony had been on his own for 10 years and Georgia, 11 years and they knew how important it was to give each other 'space to breathe', learning from previous marriages. Tony rented out his apartment and on their wedding day, Georgia gave him the keys to her flat and they shared their lives with the deepest respect and space for each other.

Thanks to Amy, her new single friend, Georgia passed the entrance exam containing some elementary arithmetic questions and was offered a job in the City of London as Finance Manager's assistant. A new start, just what she needed. It was a great job with great benefits and great people and Georgia was to have a wonderful life-changing experience when staff were asked if they would like to join the "Help A London Child Learn To Read Scheme" promoted by The Evening Standard Newspaper. 'What a nice thing to do' she thought and joined up. Once a month a handful of the staff would go to a local primary school and each sit with one of the children and help them with their reading. It was at the end of one of these reading sessions that Georgia couldn't find a pen to complete the usual small form about Aaron's (her charge) progress and simply grabbed a pen from her handbag filling in his and her name, the date and notes about Aaron's reading. She didn't even notice it was one of her calligraphy pens as she wrote in purple ink. Her writing with a calligraphic pen was pretty impressive and before she realised it, Aaron got up from his chair, walked behind her, leaned under the table like he was looking for something. "How did you do that?" he asked, pointing to her writing.

"Pardon?" she said, suddenly looking down at the purple ink on the page. "Oh, this is called Calligraphy. This is a very special pen that lets you write nicely. Would you like me to write your name in Calligraphy?" "Oh yes," Aaron replied as she tore the bottom of the paper, producing just a thin strip where she expertly wrote "Aaron" with a flourish at the end. "There" she said as he took it from her hand. He didn't speak and just walked out of the room, holding the paper tight to his chest. That image was to come back to her that night, as she tossed and turned in bed, unable to sleep. *'There is more to this'* she said to Tony before bed. *'It's obvious that some children have never seen Calligraphy before. Some parents don't even write anymore now we have computers"* continuing her line of thought. *'If we continue to show our children how to use computers, they will NEVER have to deal with mistakes, I mean REAL mistakes you have to correct, not just hit the delete button. This is why people nowadays don't understand the meaning of consequences!'*

Suddenly Georgia's Calligraphy was more than just a passion. It had a purpose and a very important one in the scheme of the world's future. Now she had to find a way of spreading the word. Handwriting... she must keep it alive!

It's the weekend and Georgia is back home and ready to open the box. It was time to open the thing in her tiny office alongside the bedroom. It had always been distinctive, like no other cardboard box. Black with a fine red border and cartoon red, green and yellow peppers on the lid. And everything's still there, just as she'd left it, twenty-four years ago, with two stickers "Georgia" and "Bedroom 2" still on the lid. The box was part of the home contents which, after being kept in storage, was transported to her new apartment after the divorce but she had abandoned it, leaving it to gather dust in the garage until now.

The box itself was irrelevant but it was easy to recognise after all these years. It was her very own time capsule and as she removed the lid she imagined how Howard Carter must have felt uncovering Tutankhamun's tomb and what had been hidden for so long. All the papers she'd wanted to keep, still intact, not a mouse dropping or paper nibble in sight. The paper manuscript, neatly typed, a very large padded envelope, sealed and in pristine condition and so much more than she had remembered. The copyright law she had learned about after the divorce, where the LETEC tutor had explained if you send a document to yourself by registered post, you could use it in a court of law to protect the contents from being copied. You could prove you were the first, as long as the seal was intact. The A3 padded envelope was still unopened and it took her a while to remember what she'd put in it, still sealed with the Post Office labels and a loose recorded delivery slip showing the tracking number, address and date. She had used this method of protection many times over for her ideas and logo designs and an invention she had been working on years ago. She'd sent herself a copy of the drawing and description. It was such a simple invention, pretty neat she thought. It could have been used as an everyday office item, but she never had the confidence to pursue it any further. Her invention would still be as useful today as it was all those years ago. If only she'd had more confidence and trust in people. Even the patent attorney she went to see was, in her eyes, too much of a risk to divulge her invention to. After all, he could easily pass the idea onto someone else and there would be no trace of dodgy dealing. The invention is still tucked away somewhere now, but it's not important anymore.

There was a video in the box. She remembered that. It was the recording Larry had made of her appearance on the morning TV show in 1996, where Georgia for the first time had gone public about her situation. The subject was Control Freaks and she remembers how Larry had set the day and time on the video recorder before they left for the TV studios in London. This was there in the box but there was one thing more important than that and she searched the papers, lifting them gently, one at a time. She'd been speaking about this for years and needed to find it to confirm it wasn't a dream. The Court Order from her mother. Yes, it was real. And harrowing. There were old family photos but she was too nervous to study them carefully and just quickly glanced at some familiar faces. The musty garage smell made everything appear as if it had come from another time and place, not ancient Egypt, but it was like a life she had left behind so long ago. It was beginning to intoxicate her and not in a good way. She could hear Tony in a panic in the lounge because the time for his online order for their new freezer was counting down and running out, which raised her anxiety levels even more. I'll return to the box when I'm feeling stronger. It was the most perfect of summer days outside anyway and he was calling to her to go outside as she began to feel suffocated by the events of the past. As she put the lid on the box she felt her new-found strength dissipate in seconds as confronting those papers from the past again brought the old feelings of insecurity and uncertainty flooding back. Again.

Photos of the girls going way back in time when they were small. Sylvie's handwritten envelopes, still insisting on spelling the address incorrectly, the magazine article about Caraline who triggered something so deep inside Georgia that was to start her writing the book in the first place. Caraline sadly losing her battle with anorexia nervosa, symptoms that had touched Georgia in her younger days. She can still hear her mother saying 'You're just looking for attention.'

And then there was the little gem, Larry's long forgotten hand-written statement in the box. It was right there, amongst the summons from the court, taped to the bottom of a carbon copy of a letter she had written to her mother's solicitor in response to the court action and in Larry's own distinctive capitalised handwriting, this priceless statement read:

*'SIMPLY BY HER OWN ACTIONS TO INVOLVE THE LEGAL PROFESSION AND TAKE HER GRIEVANCE AS FAR AS TO GO TO COURT INSTEAD OF BEING PREPARED TO LISTEN TO HER DAUGHTER FOR THE FIRST TIME IN HER LIFE AND ALSO LISTEN TO HER GRANDCHILDREN, HAS ONLY RESULTED IN OUR CHILDREN BEING PUT UNDER SUCH STRESS AND UPSET THAT SHE HAS MADE THEM FEEL EVEN STRONGER AGAINST SEEING SUCH A WOMAN, WHICH IN TURN HAS MADE MY WIFE AND ME ONLY TO REAFFIRM OUR FEELINGS THAT MRS. X HAS NO UNDERSTANDING TOWARD HER FAMILY ESPECIALLY MY WIFE, HER DAUGHTER AND HAS NOT TAKEN OUR CHILDRENS FEELINGS INTO ACCOUNT, WHICH MEANS SHE HAS ONLY TAKEN THIS ACTION FOR SELF GAIN AND SELF PITY!'*

'Ok, so that was the end of my book' she thought back in 1996, but she had no idea what was to come and THIS is where things really got interesting, especially when she saw Larry's handwritten statement. Surely this would prove her innocence and clear her name with the girls, once and for all? She could not give up on her own children. They must hear her.

# CHAPTER TWENTY-THREE

# TIMELESS VALUES

She took the old manuscript from the top of the box, closed the lid and offered Tony the typed papers she had spent 24 years preparing, now seeing daylight for the first time and he was going to be the very first person to read it. She was glad to sit in the glorious sunshine, watching the huge wood pigeons that had made their home in the communal gardens of the apartment block. She'd lived here 12 years and could still remember the day she moved in, 4th July 2003. Talk about Independence Day!

So, all these years on and after an hour, to her amazement, Tony is still reading which she finds hard to believe and is staring at him as he continues reading. "I'm enjoying it," he said as he asked "Why are you staring at me? You can write!" he said, gesturing with a wave to let him carry on. He was serious and that was a shock. 'She could write and write something of interest?' He must be biased. Yes of course he is, but he's also his own man, choosing what he likes and dislikes but she knew he wouldn't read rubbish. Wow. Her book *isn't* rubbish? She could hardly comprehend the idea. This was so surprising. Never in her wildest dreams could she imagine someone actually wanting to read her words. The truth. Tony had turned off the TV. His concentration was entirely focussed on her manuscript. She noticed how surprised and humbled she felt by his genuine interest. She felt the oppression waiting, calling her to the old days, when she had no say in any matter, but then she realised she had all the strength
ded to rise above this major player of a demon
engage with her again. 'Oh no, you won't have
e, you bastard. Now I'm armed with so much
uch more than before.

needed to say but now, the recent discoveries she had made were just the first scratch of a surface that had a very deep underbelly still to be uncovered. By page 66 she was reliving the nightmare that had been so hard to learn to cope with. She thought it couldn't touch her again but she felt the depression creeping back like an old familiar face you never want to see again. Pages 67 and beyond will have to wait until she has collected herself and found the inner strength she knows is not far away. It was there only moments ago. 'I'll start 67 soon but not today'.

It was a different time and she was a very different person now, seen on TV, teaching calligraphy around the world, working with charities, giving lectures to the public and generally making a name for herself. It was only now she was beginning to see the insignificance of this hoard she had collected and knew it was time to get rid of it all.

As she cleaned around the flat she saw books she had collected over the years, still dotted around where they'd been left in times of crisis, "Thoughts of peace," "Calm," "Timeless values," books that had given temporary comfort in such times of despair. Now the picture was emerging. She had surrounded herself and her new husband with all the aids she could find to help cope with the devastating trauma, to last what she thought would be a lifetime's sentence, and her sudden awakening to it all was shocking. Had she been through so much pain? Had she needed so much support? She had and the enormity of it all was overwhelming. The bedroom was a perfect reflection of her life. Nothing had been touched for years and as she read through more of the original manuscript, she suddenly realised her life was happening, right now. The working cruises, classes, lectures and in the middle of everything she was decorating the bedroom, putting new flooring and wallpaper in the kitchen. All because she was ready to move on and throw the old stuff away at last.

There had been only one thing that had remained constant throughout her life, and that was her Calligraphy. Everything had changed out of all recognition, including her and the world. Few people had ever taken her Calligraphy seriously but the commissions she'd received from famous companies and names gave what was to be a time capsule of her life's work, with a new-found respect. There were the memorial stones she was making, plus the artwork she was selling that hung in the local deli, everything was going her way. She was married to Tony and life felt good for the very first time in her life. She had been driven to promote Calligraphy for over 30 years and now she was dedicated to it, teaching in over 100 countries around the world. It held such importance and she was so passionate and knew it would never let her down or betray her.

## CHAPTER TWENTY-FOUR

# CONGRATULATIONS

All emails and texts between Georgia and her girls had broken down and after serious consideration of ending it all, she slowly started to build on what was left in her and began to come out of her depression. After counselling, CBT therapy, several hypnotherapy sessions and the bouts of suicidal thoughts, she slowly came to realise she had an identity of her own and although unthinkable, she could actually live a reasonably normal and happy life without her children. It had taken years to get to this point by slowly filling each waking hour with as much work as possible. Looking around, she realised how far she had come.

Constantly in her thoughts, her girls were now thirty-two and thirty-five and in the years they'd been apart there had been their weddings, births and a few deaths. Georgia was a grandmother, apparently.

Her great aunt called her one day and said "Congratulations, I hear you're going to be a grandmother." This would have been great news under normal circumstances but this was the first she had heard, not surprising as there were no members of her mother's family to tell her any news, and certainly nothing about her youngest daughter. Her aunt had only found out because Sarah had called her to thank her for the birthday card and passed on the news. Sarah did text Georgia the news that "Sophie had a baby girl today." Another well-meaning friend texted Georgia to congratulate her. Georgia texted Sophie 'Congratulations' asking her for her address so she could send flowers but just got the reply "You didn't even ask how I was." The contempt was so obvious and it still hurt.

They say you don't miss what you don't know, but Georgia did miss the chance of seeing her grandchildren. She also missed the opportunity to know and love them but she would never risk again the rejection she feared. What was the point of finding her daughter, knocking on her door to have it slammed in her face? There was only one way forward for her and that was that the girls would have to see her on her terms, which is why keeping a record of events in the book was so important.

Irony, that's a funny thing. Georgia's just found her voice when the consultant endocrinologist told her the large growth in her throat was over her thyroid gland and must be removed as *'it will only get bigger'.* Georgia had originally suspected having a heart defect after becoming short of breath for no reason, only to discover something was actually blocking her windpipe, making her gasp for air. Anyway, Miss Jenkins announced that the op would take place within the next three months, with a risk of her voice being permanently husky, possibly reduced to a whisper or gone for good after the op, but the best option was to operate sooner rather than later. Great. Just when she had important stuff to say. Georgia knew it was the constant sobbing, day and night, that created what felt like the 'brick' in her throat and somehow, again, she survived intact.

Texts were useful but so easy to misinterpret. Georgia had been desperately searching for a resolution, reconciliation, a happy ending to this nightmare with her girls and with the book too, but it was January 2016 when she woke at 5am, her best time for clear thinking, knowing there was no end in sight. But while she was alive, there was always going to be that element of hope, the tiniest glimmer of it still refusing to disappear. And the truth, the truth that will one day expose her mother's personality disorder, the good friends who tried to help and the others who just stood by, watching the hate unfold and radiate, like Larry, not wanting to do anything. Now she understands the songs and poems like Carole King's, 'You've got a friend' with the words "they'll take your soul if you let them" and this, written back in 1926:

Your children are not your children
They are the sons and daughters of life's longing for itself
They come through you but not from you
And though they are with you yet they belong not to you
You may give them your love but not your thoughts
For they have their own thoughts
You may house their bodies but not their souls
For their souls dwell in the house of tomorrow,
Which you cannot visit, not even in your dreams
You may strive to be like them but seek not to make them like you
For life goes not backward nor tarries with yesterday
You are the bows from which your children as living arrows are sent forth
The archer sees the mark upon the path of the infinite and he bends you with
His might that his arrows may go swift and far
Let your bending in the archer's hand be for gladness
For even as he loves the arrow that flies, so he loves also the bow that is stable.

**The prophet by Kahlil Gibran**

## CHAPTER TWENTY-FIVE

# GOODBYE AND HELLO

Georgia knew it was to be the very last contact she was to make with both of her children and didn't feel devastated. Her heart and head knew this was the start of something not including them. Is a happy future possible when you know you are the living, breathing, damaged result of so many family fractures?

And then she realised the most preposterous idea that was now true...... 'You cannot choose your family.' Of course you can't. But you *can* choose your friends and it's your friends who are your REAL family because you are drawn to each other, 'like attracts like.' Steering away from those she disliked, perhaps because they were purely misguided or possibly insane, Georgia was finding real warmth and genuine camaraderie with her own kind, now the minority in her world.

For some people, there is no such thing as blood-related family anymore. Simple. People like Adele in the US, who was discovered on an 'estrangement' website. Here is her story:

*"About a year ago, I was still estranged from my only daughter and my only grandkids completely, having no contact whatsoever with any of them. Although still completely crushed and heartbroken by her tossing me to the curb for fabricated reasons that she had taken to social media to slander me and her father with outright lies and unbelievable tales, I had reached the point of gradual acceptance of her abandonment and began putting the fragmented pieces of my life back together without them in it. Up to that point, as many of us on this site have done and continue to do, he had formed*

*some defence mechanisms that, whether right or wrong, seemed to help me cope with that gut-wrenching pain on which estrangement brings to each of us. Also up to that point, I had never responded to her insane accusations and allegations, instead, allowing her to continue to dig herself and her lies in deeper and deeper with each one that she told to the masses she truly believe that the longer it went on without any response from me, the angrier she became as she realized that no matter how hard she tried to provoke me to join in her childish, juvenile games, I was determined to remain unresponsive, no matter how disgustingly cruel her attempts were. In turn for my continued silence as I refused to engage in those games with her, each lie that she publicly announced to anyone that would listen became increasingly more and more vulgar in its severity and content I still refused to respond. Eventually, I guess she finally figured out that no matter what she conjured up within her own twisted and warped mind, I refused to get involved and "mix it up" with any of it or her and decided that I had had enough and was ready to go on with forming a new and hopefully happy life without her or my grands in it...period. So, the uphill battle and struggles began.*

*I took baby steps to start with, slowly getting rid of the massive collection of toys and what have you that the grands used to enjoy so much when they were still allowed to visit for regular play dates. I began remodelling and taking back the area of the house that was devoted to being a "playroom" and decided to turn it into my quilting studio instead. I very slowly began poking my head out the sand and back into an adult society after spending a couple of years deep in hiding, riddled with shame and guilt (although I knew deep inside that I had nothing about which to feel shameful or guilty) I put any hopes and dreams regarding a relationship with my daughter and grands somewhere in the back of my heart and mind and was very determined to make myself a new life that I could enjoy. So little by little, that is exactly what I did. I made up my mind, set my boundaries, deciding firmly what I would and would not tolerate with regard to the way others, all others, treated me. I would no longer associate with my daughter as long as she treated me with such disrespect and deliberate cruelty. I developed a lot of internal anger that formed a thick wall around my heart and in my head, keeping me constantly on guard and protected. My therapist said it was my defence mechanism that protected me from further pain and despair that once took me very near my own suicide. Although it may not have been entirely healthy and good, it was my only defence at the time. My therapist and I both agreed that as long as it worked, why not use it. So I did.*

*Life very slowly began to improve with fewer and fewer setbacks and triggers that sent me back into that dark, miserable, unbearable "funk" in which I was once drowning. I even began feeling stronger and more determined to emerge a better, new and improved human being, proving to everyone, especially myself, that I am not a bad mother or a bad person.*

*I am good and have lots to offer my friends and family while being that good and decent person.*

As I slowly crept my way back to life and happiness, out of the blue and without warning, I get an email from my daughter. I let it sit in my inbox for several days, unsure if I even wanted to open it and debating whether or not to just send it directly to the trash folder, never learning of its contents. Finally, curiosity got the better of me and I opened it. My daughter stated that she would like to get together with me at a nearby coffee shop for a one on one talk. To be honest, my initial thought about her email content was, "Hell NOOOO!" I felt I had come so far and refused to take another hit in the gut, thus sending me backwards. But ultimately I made up my mind to not let her offer phase me, build hope or give me good or bad feelings in general. I honestly found myself feeling absolutely nothing about her offer. I could have given a rat's ass less about the possibility of seeing her again. Had I created an empty heart within myself, now incapable of feeling emotions? Was there something wrong with me? So out of curiosity only, I accepted her invitation and arranged a meeting for an upcoming Saturday afternoon. As I had learned during the previous couple of years, anytime I had had one of our failed meetings or discussions that blew up, I was going to secretly record our little coffee date so that I would be sure not to forget or misquote anything said during our private meeting. It was a safety measure I learned to use as a defence measure for the lies and slander that often followed any discussions that I had had way back years earlier in life. My recorder had fresh batteries, my boundaries were in place and without any expectations or hope, I met her at the coffee shop for reasons not totally clear.

*When I arrived she was already there and was sitting in at a small table tucked into the corner of the shop. I grabbed a bottled water and joined her. To start with our verbal exchanges were polite, awkward and nervous, containing nothing more than the idle chit chat that one would have with a distant neighbor or friend. Finally, I blurted out, "So why have you requested this meeting?" She stated that she had been doing some thinking and wanted to try and develop a relationship with me. She wanted us to SLOWLY get to know one another again and hopefully form a loving bond between us once more. The more she spoke like this, the thicker that wall around my heart became. I never felt stronger and more determined as I thought to myself, "Don't trust a word she says woman!". See I had learned during the previous few years that my daughter did nothing or said to people unless there was something in it for her...a gain of some sort. I had learned the hard way to never trust her or anything that she said. After listening to her for a solid hour, I found myself with little to say and continued to just let her ramble on about how she could slowly build this loving relationship that she once had. She finally asked for my response to her offer. I didn't want to lower myself to her standards by saying something entirely cold and heartless. But to be very honest, I could not help but to think, "why now?", "yesterday I was a horrible, abusive, sick and twisted, sorry excuse of a mother...and today you want a relationship with me???", or "how dare you come in here actually expecting me to fall at your feet, slobbering all over you, jumping at the chance of having you rip my heart out again...you have a lot of nerve!". Instead, I quickly gathered my thoughts and said that first off, I wanted her to understand a couple* of things. I went on to say that I do not trust her and her motives. I explained that the indescribable degree of pain and despair that the previous few years had caused me, that I had made some changes in my life with regard to relationships with others and that those changes were solid and non-negotiable with ANYONE in her life. I would not tolerate dishonesty and disrespect.

I would not tip toe around her feelings, walking on eggshells so to speak. I would not live within her double standard set of rules, being scolded for stupid things such as giving the grands apple juice while allowing her in laws to freely offer and pour up gallons of the stuff in sippy cups. (Yes, that was one of many stupid things for which I was punished for...for giving her gks apple juice...what a miserable excuse of a grandparent I was...lol) And all of my stipulations were true with regard for her husband as well. I agreed that we would slowly try to build some sort of something and just see where and how it went as we went along.

I came away from that meeting feeling nothing...not a damn thing. As I parted I found myself saying the words, "I love you". But did I mean it? If I did, wouldn't I have some sort of something I would be feeling in my heart? I felt nothing...absolutely nothing. Had I built this wall around myself that had grown so hard and thick that I now was incapable of feeling at all? Nothing seemed to phase me. If anything, it made me more determined to keep that wall up and to make damn sure I kept it up. I was sure something was up her sleeve and that it was only a matter of time before she would drop the ball on me, sending me falling over the edge of insanity once more. But for now,

*I would just sit back and let this part of her game play out and see where it takes her (not me...cuz she's not taking me anywhere by God!).*

*After that meeting and feeling nothing more than nothing, I had a couple of stops to make before heading home. So by the time I arrived at my house an hour or two had passed. I pulled my phone from my purse. It showed that I had missed a couple of calls while I was out and about, especially since I had it turned off during my daughter's meeting and had not yet turned it back on. One call was from an old friend that I had not spoken with in several months and the other call was from my sister with whom I rarely speak due to some unrelated issues that I won't get into here and now. I thought, "how odd to hear from her... I wonder why" I then realized that she also left me a voice mail. So I listened to it and was shocked to hear her go on and on in that message about how happy she was to learn that my daughter and me had "kissed and made up" and were on the mend, etc., etc. What??? Where did she hear anything about anything and who the hell said that I had "kissed and made up"? It hit her almost instantly... Facebook...good ol' "nothing in life is private" Facebook. Since my daughter had blocked me from her FB a year earlier to keep me from seeing her lying slanderous posts and making sure that I would have no access to pics of the gks, I rarely looked at that website anymore. But I did that day. And what do you know, the first thing I see when entering it is a new friend request from my daughter and one from her husband. I also had a private message from the daughter wanting to know if I was free to come to their house for dinner the following day and asking if I wanted to see the grands. WHAT??? I thought, "This is what you call taking it slow?" When I had just a couple of hours ago left the coffee shop she was talking about getting together once a week or so over a cup of coffee to begin anew and take it slow. But within a couple of hours we are now up to telling the world via FB that everything is "hunky dory", you wanna see the gks and won't you please come to dinner???? The best word I could use to describe my overall feeling was CONFUSION! By then I was even more convinced that she was up to something, although I wasn't exactly sure what. So I put my guard up a notch or two and decided to play it very calm and casual and let her stew a little without responding to her message or request. The following morning I called her.*

*When she answered the first thing I said was to ask her about how her sister knew anything about our previous day's meeting and insisted on knowing what all was said. She passed it off as they had just happened to be exchanging messages in FB and that the subject of ME just happened to come up between them, blah, blah, blah. I thought to herself, "What a crock!" Then I said it...yes that is exactly what I said. But I said it with great politeness and felt absolutely no guilt about it either. Why should I? If she and her sister felt the need to gossip about me then I am sure as hell not going worry about either of them and whether or not I was being politically correct with my statements. She finally admitted that when she arrived home she put something out into social media about the two of us having a "positive" little get together and that things were looking up. I immediately said that I don't want ANY PART of anything regarding and concerning me to be broadcast on ANY social media site, period. She agreed. As far as her and her husband's FB friend requests...I let those sit unanswered for several weeks before I finally OK'd them. Her invitation to dinner? I passed on that. I felt that it was "rushing" or "forcing" something that may or may not be there. I also stated that by attending dinner at THEIR home I know myself well enough to know that it would have made me feel very caged or boxed in, trapped within their "home field advantage", which made me very uncomfortable. As far as the gks were concerned...although I was dying to see them, I was scared to death to see them also, if that makes sense.*

*See the last time I saw either of them the older girl was 4 and the younger girl was still a baby, being just about 7 months old. They were now 7 and 3...a huge difference in age at that stage in life. The older one and I were extremely close from her birth and right up to the day that my daughter threw me out of her and their lives. My gks were my pride and joy and I had play dates together just about every day up until then. I was terrified that the older one would not remember me at all or that she had been brainwashed by her parents and had been taught to dislike or even hate me. Without allowing her to hear the fear I had in my voice, I told her that I thought meeting up with the gks in a neutral place would be better for all concerned to start with. I also added that I was tied up during the upcoming several days and that any meetings would have to be scheduled after that. I guess I wanted to sound as cool as could be and give her no hint of being anxious for any relationships with any of them...*

*AKA another way of protecting myself from that sickening gut wrenching pain that I had been dealing with for a few years up until that point in time. I told her that as long as I was laying some of my cards on the table I needed to tell her that I would not and could not trust her and likely never would. I said that I would not even attempt to describe what her abandonment had done to me and my life, not to mention the life of my husband (her stepfather) and her father. There is absolutely no way that she, or any other selfish, childish, narci, self-absorbed, entitled, immature, spoiled rotten, heartless and cruel adult child bitch (yep... I said it!) could ever understand that level of pain and grief. She began crying and saying, "I know Mom, I know". I asked her to never ever say that to me again...that she knows how she hurt me...cuz she will never know that feeling or could even begin to understand what it does to a woman's very soul at the deepest of levels. She apologized. I told her that it was not my place to forgive her for anything that she may or may not have done or said to cause me such pain. Instead, she should ask for forgiveness from God since He is the one that wrote the rules..."Thou shalt honour thy father and thy mother". So she owes Him the apology. Before our call ended I also said that if somewhere down the road she decided to once again throw me to the curb, no matter what flimsy reason she may have for doing so, that that would finalize any chance for the two of us to have or ever have any type of relationship whatsoever. I advised her to make absolutely sure deep inside her head and heart that she honestly wants to attempt a real relationship with me because this would be our final try. If it didn't work out I would wash her hands 100% of her, her husband and the gks forever.*

*And I meant it with all my heart. As I have said to her repeatedly during this entire mess and said once again on the phone, I know I was not a perfect parent...and she was not a perfect kid either. I did the best I could with what I had and devoted my entire life to make sure she had it far better than I ever had it, no matter what price I had to pay to ensure her life of never going without. And whether that life she was given was perfect or not, there is nothing that anyone can do or say to change anything during that time. It is what it is and that's it. Grow up. Take responsibility for your own life since you are now 34 years old. It is about time. And I left it at that, period. I guess I took back my role as the parent while setting her back in her place as the child. I told her if she wanted to hash out over and over stupid things from the past such as "do you remember when you grounded her for....", in an attempt to create guilt by me or to fish for some sort of apology for doing my job as a parent, then she would have to take that backward journey alone. My life and its enjoyment were a top priority for me and would remain as such since I am not getting any younger these days.*

*In closing I told her I was moving forward in my own life and that I refused to back pedal for anyone or any reason. She seemed rather speechless.*

*Since then we have seen each other many times and have even done things, such as attending craft fairs and other local events together. I have begun forming new relationships with both my gks as I was very correct in thinking they would not remember me...they didn't...not at all. None of our relationships between any of us will ever be the same. I still don't trust her any further than I* can throw her and still have this great, thick wall around myself. I seriously doubt that I will ever take it down for anyone again. I don't allow myself to get too close, ever. It's just too scary to let that much go out to anyone. For now, I am trying to enjoy my life the way that I choose while keeping my mind open to the fact that at any time she could suddenly and without warning do that to me again. I guess I am just keeping myself ready in case that should ever happen. I simply cannot forget that level of pain that will never be far from my everyday thoughts. And if she doesn't like the new "hardened" Mom, then she has only her own doings to blame for it.

My advice for anyone faced with a "kiss and make up" possibility with your estranged children.... walk very lightly, keep your eyes wide open and your heart well protected. I will keep all of you posted as things develop or unravel... we will see and only time will tell.

I know I haven't posted anything on the site in quite some time, although I do visit quite often still I find it difficult to share my feelings about reconciling with many mothers that believe that to reconcile with an EC (estranged child) is all wonderful and for many, the ultimate goal in their lives. If only they knew the real truth of reconciling after years of no contact. It is actually very difficult. Allow me to explain.

We all know the pain and anguish we have all experienced from the moment that we were tossed to the curb by our own offspring...that gut wrenching heartache that sent us all to the brink of sanity, the unwarranted guilt and shame we all were forced to endure, the endless tears as our *self-worth and esteem were chiselled away inch by inch to the point of having no joy, happiness or positive aspects of our lives at all. We were all sent to bottom of that black hole where we thought we would never find a way to climb up and out of that horrible hole. I, myself, hit such a low that I questioned whether or not I even wanted to go on living or if I would be better off just putting an end to that misery by taking my own life. In all of the misfortunes and awful events that had occurred during my life and up until that point, I had always managed to pull myself up to carry on with life. I had endured things such as in 1986... within that one year I went through a divorce, lost my home, lost my job, filed bankruptcy, was hospitalized with a serious illness and had my only son pass away. After living through all of that I assumed that there was nothing I could not handle in life. I was wrong. The estrangement by my only living child several years after 1986 was far worse than that entire year of 1986.*

*I went through all the stages of grief...the sadness, the guilt, the shame, the attempts of contact, the apologizing for things that never happened or were not true, the walking on eggshells, then the bitterness, the anger, even at times the hate. But eventually, those tears washed away the fog and I was able to see more clearly and was able to make sense of some of the situation. I decided to go on with my life, without my child or my gks that had been abruptly yanked from my life. I began living my NEW normal life, little by little. I knew it would take a very long time to get to that "good place" while I got to know me all over again. As I did, I began organizing my own life and decided to begin setting my boundaries of what I would and would not tolerate from and by others with regard to the roles they played in my life. Finally, I had begun learning how to allow myself to feel a fraction of joy in my own life and depended on no one but me for that pleasure. No matter how many times my daughter would bait me, attempting to get me to engage in her childish games in an effort to draw a response from me, I refused. As hard as it was, I ignored all of her Facebook posts, emails, snide remarks she would make to others about me, the lies she would tell to the masses, etc. I ignored them all as I continued to climb upward out of that black hole and back into my own life. Eventually, her attempts became fewer and fewer and finally ceased, which was fine with me. The person that my daughter had become was nothing short of evil. I did not know the person she had become, nor did I wish to know her. I was through, done and finished.*

*As I began gaining a foot hold in life...a new life without my daughter and grandkids, I became stronger and stronger, but not to the point of being entirely strong, if that makes sense. I knew it was going to be a very long road, although one that I finally felt was at least possible. A few months after this point, out of the blue and with no warning whatsoever, my daughter sent me that message asking if we could meet at the coffee shop.*

*From the moment that I received that message, my honest first thought and emotion was absolute fear. Not fear of me. But instead fear that she could possibly hurt me once again, taking me backward to that deep, dark hole again. I knew I had gained strength over the time since she first threw me out like yesterday's trash. But did I have enough strength to NOT ALLOW her to have that type of power over me again. That I was not so sure about. So yes, the thought of meeting with her scared me to death. That is why it took me some time before I would even answer her message as to whether or not I wanted to meet with her. Eventually, as you know, I agreed and we met. But before I had that first meeting I had to spend several days preparing myself for that initial meeting, pumping myself up. I would not allow myself to become hopeful and would assume nothing would come of our meeting. But more importantly, I organized my thoughts and especially my boundaries of what I would and would not tolerate in my life. I asked myself what I expected and what I would like to gain from the meeting...of course, my wish was to reconnect with my grandkids. If it weren't for them, I honestly am not so sure I would have even responded to her request for the meeting at all. Like I said, she had grown into an evil person that I had no desire at all to know... she was no longer my daughter.*

*I approached the meeting and her very cautiously, guarding my heart very well, not trusting anything that she did or said. Over the following weeks I kept that guard up and was on my toes continually.*

*As far as where we are now and how our relationship is doing, I can honestly say that it is nothing like it was before. I still do not trust her at all and have concluded that I likely never will trust her. I had to develop all new relationships with my darling GKs. That close bond I had with them before the estrangement was gone forever. My estranged daughter stole that from me and I also know that I will never forgive her for taking that away from not only me, but from her own kids as well. That was not hers to take. It had nothing to do with her or her husband. But she took it anyway. I can find it in my heart to forgive most anything in life. But I cannot see myself ever forgiving her for that. My husband, I know for a fact, will never forgive her for it. In fact, he has a very hard time being friendly while in the same room with her. He has little love or respect for her. But I am sure that is largely due to the fact that while she was off posting her nasty and hateful lies about how she was raised in such an abusive home and environment, my husband saw how her badgering and evil behavior nearly destroyed me to the point of nearly taking my own life. She never saw that part of it, but he did. And that has left a lot of anger with him. That is understandable in my book.*

*The type of relationship I have with my daughter now feels fake, not close and phony. We are courteous to each other and get along fine. But I don't think it is anywhere near as close as it once was.. I still feel that if I had no GKs, I likely would not have any type of relationship with her. The estrangement put a permanent scar on my heart and on my soul...one that will never heal. Also, suddenly when I first started having contact once again, I believe the stress of the entire estrangement began catching up to me and my health began to waiver. One by one, I have had one health issue after another creep up on me, some very serious. I have no doubt whatsoever, although it cannot be proven, that the stress of the estrangement was a cause of those. Undoubtedly it will cut years from my life.*

*In my opinion, someone that could simply toss their own parent to the curb and go onto social media and anyone that would listen, telling such evil lies about that parent, could do it again if they wanted to repeat the process in the future. And I keep myself prepared for that "what if" by guarding my heart with iron and steel fencing. For now, I enjoy the time with my 2 beautiful GKs and take full advantage of every minute of it. My daughter? I could take her or leave her. I just cannot allow her to get to close to me. Unfortunately, in order to have a close relationship with the GKs, I have to have some sort of civil relationship with their mother too...honestly speaking.*

*My message to the mothers still hoping to reconcile with their EC??? If you do, accept from the beginning that the relationship will NEVER be the same, be careful and stick to your own personal boundaries. As the old saying goes, 'Hurt her once, shame on you. Hurt her twice, shame on me.'*

*Stay strong. I promise that things will at some point, begin to get better and you will become stronger. Some things I have read on the site I still repeat to myself over and over when I need to...*

*Your adult child made the choice to estrange you. You did not abandon that child.*

*You cannot make sense of the senseless.*

*You were and are a good parent.*

*Take care of yourself first and foremost always.*

*Refuse to be disrespected by anyone in your life ever again.*

*Love yourself and only love others in your life that appreciate you and cherish the love that you give them.*

*Don't lower yourself to the estranger's level. You are better than that.*

*Make a life for yourself once again.*

*What better revenge could you ask for than to show your estranged child that their cruelty has only made you a better and stronger human and that as hard as they may have tried to break you, you could not be broken, but instead have become an even better person than you were before.*

*Hugs and prayers are with you from me.*

*Adele"*

## CHAPTER TWENTY-SIX

# WHAT IF?

There are no 'if only's' for Adele, Georgia or anyone estranged. The loss of a living child will be felt as deeply, if not more, than the real death of a child. They will always be a part of us even though they may only be a part of our past now.

Georgia recognises and admits the pattern of her own behaviour -- afraid to say too much to her children, afraid of confrontation and rejection and attempting in her ineffective way to try and hold it all together, desperately trying to keep one indiscretion secret. Your way may have been better but we still end up with the same. Estranged.

But now there is a 'What if...?"

There are many parents' experiences like Georgia's and Adele's that could be repeated here, all with the same theme... abandonment. *Why did they suddenly stop caring for no good reason?*

Millions struggle to make sense of the sentence they have been given, apparently convicted of a crime that has no rhyme or reason behind it. Millions too ashamed or embarrassed to broach the subject with anyone other than perhaps a trusted friend.

But it doesn't have to end that way.

Historically, women have initiated more divorce proceedings than men. This is pertinent as to why so many daughters estrange their mothers. In years gone by a wife would stay with her husband for the sake of the children. As desperately unhappy as she may have been, with no security to call her own, she depended on her husband to survive and so remained, enduring whatever hardship to keep the family strong AND TOGETHER. This gave support to and from the children in troubled times and we can see how the war years made families close.

Just a few years ago in the UK, a national newspaper printed these five words as its entire front cover headline: "THIS IS NOT OUR ERA". This statement has never been more relevant when it comes to the subject of family in the twenty-first century. Many values have changed including women having no need to tolerate an unhappy marriage now, whatever the reason, as their rise over the decades in equality and independence to their partner means divorce has never been easier.

Although not all estrangements are triggered by divorce, there is growing evidence that there was most likely history of a split or fall out somewhere within the family or even hidden in the in-laws' past. An adult child can be coerced by their own partner into cutting ties, denying grandparents access to their grandchildren for seemingly no good reason. Sometimes this decision is made without any concept of the consequences it holds for those displaced. The permutations of how peoples' break ups affect others are incalculable and the true outcome is as yet unknown. Some skeletons in a family's closet may never be fully exposed and it pays to be mindful of this.

Georgia came through better at the end of her experience. Intact, sane and happy despite the childless and grandchild-less circumstances she lives with. Bad things were said to her by her children and she said bad things back to them. Georgia does not know if she will ever see or hear from her children again and in the meantime, she is considerably healthier than ever before and the conclusion she has reached about estrangement may surprise and even shock you.

It is possible that in some estrangement cases, for example in Georgia's, her children had witnessed their own parents' estrangement, i.e., mummy doesn't talk to her mummy and mummy divorced daddy. This may be so in your own case, (although you may not even know about it if it was under your radar) you may have *unknowingly* and *unwittingly* set the conditioning in action. This means we may have perpetuated our children's regard for estrangement as **normality** because we were too distressed at the time to explain to them how *abnormal* the decision to estrange was and how abhorrent it was to do such a thing, even though it may have been the only way out for us at the time.

Just a show of your anger, or telling them a truth they weren't ready to hear could be all it took for them to wield the 'e' (estrangement) because that was how they perceived dealing with things they didn't like or couldn't cope with.

An unimportant problem to us may mean much more to our children and having been shown how to deal with a member of the family (or even a stranger somewhere back in time) that has upset them is how they have learnt how to deal with unpleasantries. It is human nature for children to copy their parents and as long as we can truly justify our actions at the time, whether it was to divorce or estrange someone in our life, we have no choice but to accept the outcome of that action. We must learn to suspend judgement. Our children are blameless. There is no right or wrong ruling for those responsible for the estrangement.

Even though we know 'e' is anything but normal, it has a very different meaning to our children. We may never get the chance to explain how monumental our decision to estrange a family member was or why we divorced our partner. We may never be able to explain how big a deal it still is for us to make our voice heard, whatever caused the initial hurt.

By the very nature of 'e,' explaining this to an estranged adult child is never going to be easy, if not impossible. And if the child experiences their parents' divorce, however legitimate the reasons were at the time, that child was witness to our decision. We cannot deny our own actions and the only thing we can do is try and explain the reason if, of course, we get the chance. If that chance is gone we can only accept facts that are hard to face... like years ago when we were young and imagined what it would be like to have children and grandchildren of our own, enjoying those rich relationships just as we had. We never expected our children could or would cut us out of the plans we had. Our dreams to share our life with them and our grandchildren may simply not be important enough for them. They had their reasons and may have excluded you before you could find out what those reasons were. Their priorities are not the same as ours. This is evolution.

Even Adele admits:

*"… referring to a significant other leaving the family and the affected person excusing that absent person by saying "but that's ok"….I never really considered how that may possibly contribute to our own kids' thoughts that "it's OK to abandon or disassociate one's self from a family unit. Thinking back, I am quite sure that I probably mentioned a time or two to my own daughter over the years how my father left our family when I was young, vanishing from our lives completely, and how that was "OK"…..BUT…that's OK…" statement at the end, excusing his absence as though it WAS truly OK. So…maybe I was a contributor to my daughter's way of thinking that it was perfectly OK to dump your parents whenever you want or for whatever reason you may have."*

It is a regret many might share and despite an awful price to pay, in time we can learn to accept what we did and move on with life without our children. After 13 years of no children or grandchildren in Georgia's life, accepting what was, without doubt, her own making is the only conclusion that makes sense in such a senseless situation. It may be yours too.

However hard we try and rid ourselves of it, conditioning WILL condition us. If we cannot be heard and listened to or we simply get dismissed like an old shoe, we will have to learn to recognise and deal with anything 'family' related we encounter throughout our lives in a new way. There is a time to use 'e' but just not when significant people in our lives are involved unless we can make it crystal clear that what we did was *not normal*. We can live in hope that there will someday be a reconciliation but not at the cost of believing in ourselves. Despite the loss of our children feeling like a living bereavement we must not let our own lives and that of Caraline Neville Lister, ever be in vain.

There is only one way that will work for us all in this awful predicament:

We must:

- be scrupulously honest with ourselves
- not be deluded
- accept what has happened and what we still have
- stop waiting to start living.

*"WHAT WE DO NOW ECHOES IN ETERNITY"*
Marcus Aurelius 121–180ce

# AFTERWORD

# LET'S GET THIS THING MOVING

There are no words that can describe the pain of family estrangement and not everyone suffering this loss is a celebrity. This a global issue that affects ordinary folk like you and me. Anti-depressants, drugs, alcohol, even therapy can only provide temporary relief with no real chance of alleviating the emotional pain of this awful condition. Acceptance by those abandoned and the general public alike is the only way forward for a life worth living.

Global understanding and support for sufferers is what is needed and you can help by creating your own support group. Help open up this subject to the public because, chances are, they are suffering just like you

Despite family estrangements growing around the world, it is still generally regarded by many as a taboo subject, so the more we can bring it out into the open, the less pain or shame we will feel about it.

I am gathering others' estranged stories to be published in a new book and if you would like to share your experience please send it to sandygrayson11@gmail.com with your express permission to publish and I will add it to the ever-expanding evidence of this global affliction.

I am looking forward to hearing from you.

With my best wishes, keep safe and be happy.

You're worth it, you'll see.

Sandy Grayson

Made in the USA
Middletown, DE
05 December 2022

17143111R00130